BASIC GRAMMAR and USAGE

ALTERNATE EDITION

ISBN: 0-15-504928-3

Library of Congress Catalog Card Number: 79-90862

Printed in the United States of America

BASIC GRAMMAR and USAGE

ALTERNATE EDITION

Penelope Choy

Los Angeles City College

Harcourt Brace Jovanovich, Inc.

New York San Diego Chicago San Francisco Atlanta
London Sydney Toronto

Preface

Basic Grammar and Usage, Alternate Edition, is a new form of the original edition. The explanatory portions of the text are only slightly changed, but most of the examples within the text and all the exercises are new. The tests in the Instructor's Manual are also new.

The book that eventually developed into *Basic Grammar and Usage* was originally written for students in a special admissions program at the University of California, Los Angeles. As part of their participation in the program, the students were enrolled in a composition and grammar course designed to prepare them for the university's freshman English courses. When the program began in 1971, none of the grammar textbooks then on the market seemed suitable for the students, whose previous exposure to grammar had been cursory or, in some cases, nonexistent. As the director of the program's English classes, I decided to write a book of my own that would cover the most important areas of grammar and usage in a way that would be easily understood by my students.

The original version of *Basic Grammar and Usage* received an enthusiastic response from the students and was used successfully throughout the three-year duration of the program. After the program ended in 1974, many of the instructors asked permission to reproduce the book for use in their new teaching positions. By the time copies of *Basic Grammar and Usage* reached Harcourt Brace Jovanovich, the text had already been used by more than 1,500 students in nearly a dozen schools.

Basic Grammar and Usage presents material in small segments so that students can master a particular topic one step at a time. The lessons within each unit are cumulative. For example, students doing the pronoun exercises for Lesson 11 will find that those exercises include a review of the constructions treated in Lessons 8 to 10. This approach reinforces the students' grasp of the material and helps them develop the skills they need for the writing of compositions. To make them more interesting to students, the exercises in four of the six units are presented in short narratives rather than as lists of unrelated sentences. Each lesson concludes with two exercises, which may be either used in class or assigned as homework. In addition, each unit ends with a composition that the students must proofread for errors and then correct to demonstrate mastery of the material.

Students who have never before studied grammar systematically will find that working through the text from beginning to end provides an insight into the basic patterns of English grammar. As one student commented on an end-of-course evaluation, "The most important thing I learned from *Basic Grammar and Usage* is that if you learn what an independent clause is, half of your grammar problems are over." On the other hand, students who do not need a total review of grammar can concentrate on the specific areas in which they have weaknesses. To help the instructor evaluate both types of student, the Instructor's Manual accompanying the text includes a diagnostic test and a post-test divided into sections corresponding to the units in the book. There are also separate achievement tests for each unit, as well as answer keys to the exercises presented in the text.

Although *Basic Grammar and Usage* is designed for students whose native language is English, it has been used successfully by students learning English as a second language. In addition to being a classroom text, *Basic Grammar and Usage* can be used in writing labs and for individual tutoring.

I would like to thank the people at Harcourt Brace Jovanovich who have participated in the publication of the Alternate Edition of *Basic Grammar and Usage*: Eben W. Ludlow, who sponsored the original edition; Natalie Bowen, my manuscript editor; Jean T. Davis, my copy editor; Nancy Margolis, the compositor for both editions; and, most of all, Bill McLane, my present editor, whose continual encouragement and indefatigable optimism enabled this book to be written.

Penelope Choy

Table of Contents

Identifying Subjects and Verbs

1 Sentences with One Subject and One Verb

The most important grammatical skill you can learn is how to identify subjects and verbs. Just as solving arithmetic problems requires you to know the multiplication tables perfectly, solving grammatical problems requires you to identify subjects and verbs with perfect accuracy. This is not as difficult as it sounds. With practice, recognizing subjects and verbs will become as automatic as knowing that 2 x 2 = 4.

Although in conversation people often speak in short word groups which may not be complete sentences, in written English people usually use complete sentences.

A complete sentence contains at least one subject and one verb.

A sentence can be thought of as a statement describing an *actor* performing a particular *action*. For example, in the sentence "The man fell," the *actor* or person performing the action is the *man*. What *action* did the man perform? He *fell*. This *actor-action* pattern can be found in most sentences. Can you identify the actor and the action in each of the sentences below?

The Dodgers lost.
I opened the book.

The *actor* in a sentence is called the **subject**. The *action* word in a sentence is called the **verb**. Together, the subject and verb form the core of the sentence. Notice that even if extra words are added to the two sentences above, the subject-verb core in each sentence remains unchanged.

The *Dodgers lost* the 1978 World Series to the New York Yankees.
I opened the book to the assignment on page 12.

You can see that in order to identify subjects and verbs, you must be able to separate these core words from the rest of the words in the sentence.

Here are some suggestions to help you identify subjects.

1. The subject of a sentence is usually a **noun** or a **subject pronoun**. A **noun** is the name of a person, place, or thing, such as *Tom, Chicago,* or *pencils.* A noun may also be the name of an abstract idea, such as *happiness* or *success.* A **subject pronoun** is a word used in place of a noun, such as *he* (= *Tom*) or *they* (= *pencils*). Underline the subjects of the following sentences:

   The store opens at ten o'clock.

   We live in Chicago.

   Ralph works twenty hours a week.

   Minnesota has very cold winters.

2. **Adjectives**—words which describe a noun—are *not* part of the subject. For example, in the sentence "The blue Volkswagen belongs to me," the subject is "Volkswagen," *not* "blue Volkswagen," because "blue" is an adjective describing "Volkswagen." In the sentence "The antique car costs thirty thousand dollars," the subject is "car," *not* "antique car." Underline the subjects of the following sentences.

   The famous boxer retired for the third time.

   The Cuban restaurant serves black beans and rice.

3. Words that show **possession**, or ownership, are *not* part of the subject. Words that show possession include nouns ending in an apostrophe combined with "s," such as *Larry's* or *store's.* They also

include **possessive pronouns**, words that replace nouns showing ownership, such as *his* (= *Larry's*) or *its* (= *store's*). The words *my, your, his, her, its, our,* and *their* are possessive pronouns. Thus, in the sentence "My father retired last year," the subject is "father," *not* "my father." In the sentence "Gordon's friend prepared the meal," the subject is "friend," *not* "Gordon's friend." Underline the subjects of the following sentences:

Mary's kite rose higher and higher.

His class meets three times a week.

My friend's husband fixed my car.

4. In **commands**, such as "Shut the door!", the subject is understood to be the subject pronoun *you* even though the word *you* is almost never included in the command. *You* is understood to be the subject of the following commands:

Answer the phone!
Please help me

Underline the subjects of the following sentences. If the sentence is a command, write the subject *you* in parentheses at the beginning of the sentence.

Fresh fruit makes a good dessert.

She enjoys good music.

My neighbor's car blocked my driveway.

Please listen carefully.

You owe me five dollars.

Now that you can identify subjects, here are some suggestions to help you to identify verbs.

1. Verbs include action words, such as *hate, hit,* or *drive.* They also include all the forms of the verb *be—am, is, are, was, were,* and *been—*and other verbs, such as *seem, feel, become,* and *appear,* which can be used as substitutes for forms of *be.* These verbs are

called **linking verbs.** Underline the subject in each of the following sentences *once*, and underline the verb *twice*.

I am nervous about my final grade.

Joan seems nervous today.

He becomes nervous during tests.

2. Verbs are the only words which change their spelling to show **tense.** Tense is the time—present, past, or future—at which the verb's action occurs. For example, the sentence "They *walk* to school" has a present-tense verb. In the sentence "They *walked* to school," the verb is in the past tense. Underline the subject in each of the following sentences *once* and the verb *twice*.

Linda enjoys her job.

We enjoyed the movie.

My children eat a good breakfast every morning.

Yesterday I ate a pizza for lunch.

The Johnsons go to Europe every summer.

Last summer they went to Spain.

3. An **infinitive**—the combination of the word *to* plus a verb, such as *to walk* or *to study*—is *not* considered part of the verb in a sentence. Read the following sentences.

Sue needs to save money.
They want to help you.

The verbs in these two sentences are *needs* and *want.* The infinitives *to save* and *to help* are *not* included. In the following sentences, underline the subjects *once* and the verbs *twice*.

I have to find a new job.

The swimmer tried to win the race.

4. Just as adjectives are not part of the subject, **adverbs**—words which describe a verb—are not part of the verb. Many commonly used adverbs are formed by adding the ending *-ly* to adjectives.

Adjectives	*Adverbs*
slow	slowly
quiet	quietly
cheerful	cheerfully
simple	simply

The words *not, never,* and *very* are also adverbs. Like other adverbs, these words are *not* part of the verb. In the following sentences, underline the subjects *once* and the verbs *twice*.

He never remembers my phone number.

The burglar quietly entered the house.

You certainly understand this lesson.

The professor spoke very rapidly.

The repairmen are not here today.

Here is a final suggestion for identifying subjects and verbs.

It is usually a good practice to identify the verb in a sentence before you try to identify the subject.

A sentence may have many nouns and pronouns, any of which might be the subject, but it will usually have only one or two verbs. For example:

The owner of the store frequently gives students a special discount on his merchandise.

There are five nouns in the above sentence (*owner, store, students, discount, merchandise*), any of which might be the subject. However, there is only one verb—*gives*. Once you have identified the verb as *gives*, all you have to ask yourself is, "Who or what gives?" The answer is *owner*, which is the subject of the sentence.

In the following sentences, underline the subjects *once* and the verbs *twice*, remembering to locate the verb before you look for the subject.

My trip through Spain lasted for five weeks.

He bought a new stereo last month.

The football team practices every afternoon.

Remember these basic rules:

1. The person or thing performing the action in a sentence is the **subject.**

2. The action which is being performed is the **verb.**

3. A complete sentence consists of an *actor* performing an *action* or, in other words, a **subject** plus a **verb.**

In the following sentences, underline the subjects *once* and the verbs *twice.* Apply the rules which you have learned in this lesson. Do *not* make random guesses.

The store's month-end sale attracts hundreds of customers.

·He called a repairman to fix his television.

The school's playground is dirty.

Be careful with that knife.

Jean usually drives carefully.

He never wants to work on weekends.

EXERCISE 1A

Underline the subject of each sentence *once* and the verb *twice*. Each sentence has one subject and one verb. *Remember to look for the verb first* before you try to locate the subject.

1. Anatomy studies the structure of the body.

2. Grammar describes the structure of a language.

3. Every language has its own grammatical structure.

4. For example, Italians say "the my house white" (*la mia casa bianca*), not "my white house."

5. You already know most of the structures of English grammar.

6. However, some structures create special problems for composition students.

7. Perhaps your compositions contain fragments or agreement errors or mistakes in punctuation.

8. This textbook shows you how to avoid these and other kinds of errors.

9. Each lesson explains the rules for a particular grammatical structure.

10. The author provides many examples to illustrate each rule.

11. Each chapter also contains exercises.

12. The exercises allow you to measure your progress.

EXERCISE 1B

Underline the subject of each sentence *once* and the verb *twice*. Each sentence has one subject and one verb. *Remember to look for the verb first* before you try to locate the subject.

1. California has millions of acres of brush-covered hills.

2. Brush fires are a serious problem during the dry summer months.

3. Each year the state uses a variety of techniques (bulldozing, controlled burning, and herbicides) to clear some of the land.

4. However, these methods cost the state a great deal of money.

5. Now a cheaper solution seems possible.

6. Goats love to eat the shrubs on California's hillsides.

7. One goat eats enough to keep two acres of land clear of brush.

8. These animals even repay the price of their own purchase.

9. For example, angora goats produce approximately sixty dollars worth of mohair per year.

10. Other goats provide meat or milk.

11. California law requires homeowners in canyon areas to keep their property free of brush and weeds.

12. A goat rental service is available for these people.

13. The homeowner pays eleven dollars a week to rent a pair of goats.

14. Two goats consume all the weeds and brush in a 100-square-foot area in two weeks.

15. They also make excellent pets.

2 Multiple Subjects and Verbs

Some sentences have more than one subject. Others have more than one verb. Many sentences have more than one subject *and* more than one verb. The subjects in the following sentences have been labeled with an "S" and the verbs with a "V."

```
S      V                    V
```
Phil washed his car and then waxed it.

```
      S      S    V
```
My neighbor and I often jog together.

```
      S        V                        S      V
```
The landlord repainted our apartment, but he also raised the rent.

```
                        S      V                          S
```
Because the television series attracted very few viewers, the network

```
V
```
canceled it.

You can identify the pattern of a sentence by indicating how many subjects and verbs it has. Although in theory a sentence can have any number of subjects and verbs, the most common patterns are:

S-V	one subject and one verb
S-V-V	one subject and two verbs
S-S-V	two subjects and one verb
S-V/S-V	two subjects and two verbs

Underline the subjects of the following sentences *once* and the verbs *twice*.

The fire destroyed several homes.

Ron saved his money for a year and then bought a new car.

A sore throat and a fever are symptoms of a cold.

New York is an exciting city, but Los Angeles has better weather.

Any group of words which contains *at least one subject and one verb* is called a **clause**. Therefore, any sentence with one S-V, S-V-V, or S-S-V pattern contains one clause. Sentences which contain only one clause are called **simple sentences**.

Sentences which contain more than one clause (each with its own subject and verb) are known as either **compound** or **complex sentences**, depending upon the kind of word which is used to join the clauses. You will study compound and complex sentences in detail in later lessons, but at the present time the important thing for you to learn is how to identify *all* the subjects and verbs in a sentence which has more than one clause.

The clauses in compound and complex sentences are joined by words called **conjunctions**. A conjunction (from a Latin word meaning "to join together") is a word that joins words or groups of words—such as the clauses you are now studying. The following conjunctions are used to join clauses in **compound sentences**:

> and   but   for   nor   or   so   yet

A compound sentence must have at least *two* subjects and *two* verbs, usually arranged in an S-V/S-V pattern. The conjunction comes in the middle of the two clauses. For example:

S   V   S   V
I wrote a letter to my friend, *but* she never answered it.

$$\overset{s}{\text{The earthquake}} \overset{v}{\text{shook}} \text{ our house, } and \text{ several } \overset{s}{\text{windows}} \overset{v}{\text{cracked}}.$$

Underline *all* the subjects *once* and *all* the verbs *twice* in the following compound sentences:

She won a supermarket contest, and her prize was a trip to Hawaii.

The sky looks clear, but the weatherman predicts rain.

I went to Spain last summer, for I wanted to improve my Spanish.

Pay the fine, or go to jail.

The supervisor is not friendly, nor is he very helpful.

The football team lost all of its games this season, so the college fired the coach.

I followed the recipe carefully, yet the cake tasted horrible.

(Are you remembering to look for the verb in each clause first?)

There are several types of **complex sentences**, and each type uses different conjunctions. The conjunctions which are used in the following sentences describe *time, place, reason,* and *condition.*

$$Whenever \overset{s}{\text{I}} \overset{v}{\text{take}} \text{ a shower, the } \overset{s}{\text{phone}} \overset{v}{\text{rings}}.$$

$$\text{The } \overset{s}{\text{puppy}} \overset{v}{\text{follows}} \text{ the child } wherever \overset{s}{\text{he}} \overset{v}{\text{goes}}.$$

$$\overset{s}{\text{We}} \overset{v}{\text{grow}} \text{ our own vegetables } because \overset{s}{\text{we}} \overset{v}{\text{want}} \text{ to save money.}$$

$$Although \overset{s}{\text{he}} \overset{v}{\text{diets}} \text{ constantly, } \overset{s}{\text{he}} \text{ never } \overset{v}{\text{loses}} \text{ weight.}$$

Some of the conjunctions used in the type of complex sentence discussed in this lesson are:

time after, at, before, until, when, whenever, while

place where, wherever

reason   because, since, so that (*not* "so")

condition   although, even though, if, unless

Notice that the conjunction may come before the first clause, as in:

$$\overset{S \quad V}{\textit{When I get home from work,}} \quad \overset{S \quad V}{\textit{I take a nap.}}$$

Or it may come before the second clause:

$$\overset{S \quad \quad V}{\textit{We gave Mr. Bronson a watch}} \quad \overset{S \quad \quad V}{\textit{when he retired.}}$$

Underline *all* the subjects *once* and *all* the verbs *twice* in the following complex sentences. Notice that each sentence contains at least *two* subjects and *two* verbs in an S-V/S-V pattern.

We waited for you for an hour before we left.

Since strawberries give Paula hives, she never eats them.

I know where the party is.

Even though cigarettes irritate his throat, Jerry continues to smoke.

EXERCISE 2A

Underline the subjects of the following sentences *once* and the verbs *twice*. Remember not to include infinitives as part of the verb. To help you, the pattern of each sentence is indicated in parentheses.

1. This story is an old Asian folktale about a mirror. (S-V)

2. It occurs, with variations, in Chinese, Japanese, and Korean literature. (S-V)

3. Long ago, mirrors were rare objects in Asia, and few people owned them. (S-V/S-V)

4. Since most people never saw a mirror, they never understood its function. (S-V/S-V)

5. However, a handsome young farmer wanted a mirror because he took pride in his appearance. (S-V/S-V)

6. Therefore, he brought a mirror home and hid it in his bedroom closet. (S-V-V)

7. Everyday he admired his reflection in the mirror for hours at a time. (S-V)

8. One day his wife noticed his actions and became suspicious. (S-V-V)

9. While her husband worked in the fields, she looked into the closet. (S-V/S-V)

10. When she saw a face in the mirror, she began to cry. (S-V/S-V)

11. "My husband has a new wife, and he keeps her here in his closet!" (S-V/S-V)

12. Her mother-in-law heard the noise and rushed into the room. (S-V-V)

13. The old woman peeked into the closet, and she too saw a face in the mirror. (S-V/S-V)

14. She jumped back in surprise. (S-V)

15. "Now I not only have a new daughter-in-law, but her mother lives here too!" (S-V/S-V)

EXERCISE 2B

Underline the subjects of the following sentences *once* and the verbs *twice*. Some sentences may have more than one subject, more than one verb, or both. Remember to look for the verbs first.

1. A favorite attraction for tourists in San Francisco is the cable car.

2. Andrew Hallidie built the first cable car in 1873.

3. Before that time, horses pulled streetcars up and down the hills of the city.

4. The horses sometimes slipped on the steep slopes, and the streetcars rolled down the hill.

5. These accidents often injured both the animals and the passengers on the streetcars.

6. Hallidie's car needed no horses because it hooked onto a cable.

7. A central steam plant provided the power to move the cable.

8. On August 1, 1873, Hallidie tested his first cable car on Clay Street, a hill with a twenty percent grade.

9. When the car's driver looked down the steep incline, he lost his courage.

10. He refused to handle the car, so Hallidie drove it himself.

11. The car moved smoothly down the hill at a speed of four miles per hour.

12. Hallidie's experiment was a great success, and soon his cars operated throughout the city.

13. In 1964 the entire cable car system became an official national historic landmark.

14. Today only three cable car lines remain, for buses, trolleys, and subways provide more efficient transportation. (This sentence has an S-V/S-S-S-V pattern.)

15. But tourists and many native San Franciscans still prefer to ride the cable cars.

3 Distinguishing Between Objects of Prepositions and Subjects

One of the most common causes of errors in identifying the subject of a sentence is confusing it with a noun used as the object of a preposition. To avoid making this type of mistake, you first must learn to recognize prepositions and prepositional phrases.

Prepositions are the short words in our language which show the *position* of one object in relation to another. For example, if you were trying to describe where a particular book was located, you might say:

The book is *on* the desk.
The book is *in* the drawer.
The book is *by* the table.
The book is *under* the notebook.
The book is *behind* him.

The italicized words are all prepositions. They show the position of the book in relation to the desk, the drawer, the table, the notebook, and him.

Here is a list of some of the most common prepositions. You do not have to memorize these words, but you must be able to recognize them as prepositions when you see them.

about	beside	of
above	between	on
across	by	onto
after	concerning	over
against	down	through
along	during	to
amid	except	toward
among	for	under
around	from	up
at	in	upon
behind	into	with
below	like	within
beneath	near	without

As you can see from the sentences describing the location of the book, prepositions are not used by themselves; they are always placed in front of a noun or pronoun. The noun or pronoun following the preposition is called the **object of the preposition**. The group of words containing the prepositions and its object is called a **prepositional phrase**. Any words, such as adjectives or the words "a," "an," or "the," which come between the preposition and its object are also part of the prepositional phrase. Read the following sentences, in which the prepositional phrases are italicized. Notice that each prepositional phrase begins with a preposition and ends with a noun or pronoun.

She reached *into her purse.*
The glasses are *on the top shelf.*
The driver *behind me* honked his horn loudly.
A cup *of coffee* costs fifty cents.

Some prepositional phrases may have more than one object.

The clerk handed the packages *to my friend and me.*
The janitor scrubbed the floor *with Spic and Span and ammonia.*

It is also possible to have two or more prepositional phrases in a row.

The television set is *in the middle of the room.*
On the way to work in the morning, I had a flat tire.

Circle the prepositional phrases in the following sentences.

The jogger ran briskly around the block.

My cousin sat beside my husband and me at the wedding.

Sue's house is near the beach in Malibu.

We went to the party with our neighbors.

Construct sentences of your own containing prepositional phrases. Use the prepositions listed below. Make certain that each of your sentences contains at least one subject and one verb.

with: _____

_____

through: _____

_____

by: _____

_____

of: _____

_____

at: _____

_____

The words "before" and "after" may be used either as prepositions or as conjunctions (p. 12). If the word is being used as a preposition, it will be followed by a noun or pronoun object. If the word is being used as a conjunction, it will be followed by both a subject and a verb.

As a Preposition

I go to bed *before midnight.*

Bob entered the room *after me.*

As a Conjunction

S   V
Before you leave the house, be sure to lock the door.

S   V
After the bell rang, the students left the room.

What do prepositional phrases have to do with identifying subjects and verbs? The answer is simple.

Any word which is part of a prepositional phrase cannot be the subject or the verb of a sentence.

This rule works for two reasons:

Any noun or pronoun in a prepositional phrase must be the object of the preposition, and the object of a preposition cannot also be a subject.

and

Prepositional phrases never contain verbs.

To see how this rule can help you to identify subjects and verbs, read the following seventeen-word sentence:

At the height of the rush hour, my car stalled in the middle of a busy intersection.

If you want to find the subject and verb of this sentence, you know that they will not be part of any of the sentence's prepositional phrases. So, first cross out all the prepositional phrases in the sentence.

~~At the height of the rush hour~~, my car stalled ~~in the middle of a busy intersection.~~

You now have only three words left out of the original seventeen, and you know that the subject and verb must be within these three words. What are the subject and verb? (Do you remember why *my* cannot be the subject?)

Read the following sentence, and cross out all of its prepositional phrases.

In the evening she works on her assignments for the next day.

If you crossed out all the prepositional phrases, you should be left with only two words—the subject *she* and the verb *works*.

Identify the subject and the verb of the following sentence.

In Southern California most of the rain falls between October and March.

If you identified all the prepositional phrases, you should be left with only two words—*most* and *falls*. Which of these words is the subject? Which is the verb?

Now you can see another reason why it is important to be able to identify prepositional phrases. It might *seem* logical for the subject of the sentence to be *rain*. However, since *of the rain* is a prepositional phrase, *rain* cannot be the subject. Instead, the subject is *most*.

Underline the subjects of the following sentences *once* and the verbs *twice*. Remember to cross out the prepositional phrases first.

Many members of Congress are lawyers.

During the oil shortage, the gas station often had no unleaded gas.

The car with the dented fender belongs to Carolyn.

A house in Beverly Hills with three bedrooms and two baths sells for two hundred thousand dollars.

All of the stores open at ten in the morning.

Underline the subjects *once* and the verbs *twice* in the following compound and complex sentences. Cross out prepositional phrases first.

The effect of television becomes apparent when students in a third grade class spell the word "relief" *R-o-l-a-i-d-s*.

The location of the shop makes it inconvenient for shoppers, so the amount of its business is very small.

EXERCISE 3A

Underline the subjects of the following sentences *once* and the verbs *twice*. Some sentences may have more than one subject, more than one verb, or both. *Remember to cross out prepositional phrases first.*

1. A cave in Altamira, Spain, contains some of the world's finest Paleolithic (Old Stone Age) paintings.

2. The twelve-year-old daughter of a Spanish archaeologist discovered the paintings by accident in 1879.

3. While her father dug in the floor of the cave for animal bones and stone tools, Maria wandered to another part of the cave.

4. On the ceiling and walls of the cave, she noticed pictures of many different kinds of animals.

5. Maria Sautuola was the first person to see these paintings in more than 15,000 years.

6. Altamira became the first of many discoveries of prehistoric cave paintings in Spain and France.

7. In Altamira, figures of bison, boars, and deer in red, brown, black, and yellow cover portions of the cave.

8. In many cases, the artists painted over natural projections in the rock, and the shape of the animals follows the contours of the stone.

9. The use of this technique gives the animals an amazingly three-dimensional and lifelike quality.

10. Historians sometimes call Altamira "the Sistine Chapel of the Ice Age" because of the beauty of its art.

11. Unfortunately, the Spanish government closed Altamira to the public several years ago.

12. Warmth from the bodies of thousands of visitors, along with the heat from electric lamps, allowed a fungus to grow in the cave.

13. The fungus threatened to destroy the paintings.

14. However, an exact replica of part of Altamira is in the National Archaeological Museum in Madrid, and tourists still visit cave paintings in many other parts of Spain.

EXERCISE 3B

Underline the subjects of the following sentences *once* and the verbs *twice*. Some sentences may have more than one subject, more than one verb, or both. *Remember to cross out prepositional phrases first.*

1. Morocco is in northern Africa, across the Strait of Gibraltar from southern Spain.

2. Each of the towns in Morocco has its own native marketplace.

3. Part of the marketplace consists of small shops with displays of brass dishes, leather goods, or rugs.

4. The owner stands at the doorway of his shop and calls to each passerby.

5. A variety of languages fills the marketplace since many shopkeepers speak French and Spanish as well as Arabic.

6. No set price exists for any item in the shop because the shopkeeper and the customer bargain with each other.

7. Eventually both of the people agree on a price, but in reality the shopkeeper always makes a profit.

8. In addition to the shops, many kinds of food fill open-air stalls along the winding streets of the marketplace.

9. Baskets of enormous fruits and vegetables attract the eyes of many shoppers.

10. Dozens of Moroccan spices, from chili peppers to cinammon, are on view in other stalls.

11. One of the most interesting stalls sells sacks of grain.

12. Each sack bears the label "A gift from the people of the United States. Not for sale."

4 Main Verbs and Helping Verbs

Verbs can be either **main verbs** or **helping** (also called **auxiliary**) **verbs**. Main verbs are the kind of verb you have already studied. Main verbs tell what action is being performed in a sentence. For example:

I *drive* to work each day.
This restaurant *serves* Mexican food.

Helping verbs are used in combination with main verbs. They perform two major functions:

1. Helping verbs indicate shades of meaning which cannot be expressed by a main verb alone. Consider the differences in meaning in the following sentences, in which the helping verbs have been italicized.

    I *may* marry you soon.
    I *must* marry you soon.
    I *should* marry you soon.
    I *can* marry you soon.

As you can see, changing the helping verb changes the meaning of the entire sentence. These differences in meaning could not be expressed simply by using the main verb *marry* alone.

2. Helping verbs also show tense—the time at which the action of the verb takes place. Notice how changing the helping verb in the following sentences changes the tense of the main verb *visit*. (Both the helping and the main verbs have been italicized.)

> He *is visiting* New York now.
> He *will visit* New York in the future.
> He *has visited* New York in the past.

Notice the position that helping verbs have in a sentence. They always *come before* the main verb although sometimes another word, such as an adverb, may come between the helping verb and the main verb.

> The team *can win* the game.
> The team *can* probably *win* the game.
> You *should* stay in bed today.
> You *should* definitely *stay* in bed today.

If a question contains a helping verb, the helping verb still comes *before* the main verb.

> *Can* the team *win* the game?
> *Should* you *stay* in bed today?
> *Does* the car *run* well?
> When *is* the plane *departing*?

The following words are helping verbs. *Memorize them.*

> can, could
>
> may, might, must
>
> shall, should
>
> will, would

The following words can be used either as helping verbs or as main verbs. They are helping verbs if they are used in combination with a main verb. They are main verbs if they occur alone. *Memorize them.*

> has, have, had   (forms of the verb *have*)

| does, do, did, done | (forms of the verb *do*) |
| am, is, are, was, were, been | (forms of the verb *be*) |

As Main Verbs	**As Helping Verbs**
He *has* my book.	He *has gone* home.
She *did* a headstand.	She *did* not *arrive* on time.
We *are* hungry.	We *are eating* soon.

From now on, whenever you are asked to identify the verbs in a sentence, *include all the main verbs and all the helping verbs*. For example, in the sentence "We should review this lesson," the complete verb is "should review." In the sentence "He has lost his wallet," the verb is "has lost." Underline the complete verbs in the following sentences.

Gail must borrow some money.

I may go to Hawaii this summer.

Sheila can speak German fluently.

We are leaving soon.

Some sentences may contain more than one helping verb.

one helping verb	The mechanic *is working* on your car.
two helping verbs	He *must have lost* your phone number.
three helping verbs	That bill *should have been paid* by now.

Underline the subjects of the following sentences *once* and the complete verbs *twice*.

You could have sold your car for a better price.

The weather will be getting warmer soon.

You have not been listening to me.

Do you have a part-time job?

Remember this rule:

The verbs in a sentence include all the main verbs plus all the helping verbs.

EXERCISE 4A

Underline the subjects of the following sentence *once* and the complete verbs *twice*. Some sentences may have more than one subject, more than one set of verbs, or both. Remember to cross out prepositional phrases first.

1. Through the ages, many different kinds of materials have been used for writing.

2. People had begun to write long before paper was invented.

3. The ancient Sumerians were writing on clay tablets as early as 4000 B.C.

4. These tablets must have been difficult to handle and to store.

5. The ancient Egyptians made their writing material from the papyrus plant.

6. The stalks of the papyrus were cut into slices, soaked, and pressed into flat sheets.

7. Sheets of papyrus could be rolled into scrolls for convenient storage.

8. The Greeks and Romans used papyrus too, but they also wrote on wooden tablets.

9. The tablets were covered with wax, and the words were cut into the wax with a sharp stylus.

10. The first real paper was invented in China in A.D. 105.

11. Fibers from the inner bark of mulberry trees were pounded into thin sheets of paper.

12. This technique for the production of paper spread first to the Arabs and then to the Europeans.

13. Paper was manufactured in Europe for the first time in Spain in 1150.

14. (Spain had previously been conquered by the Arabs.)

15. For many centuries, paper was rare and expensive.

16. Today, most paper is made from wood pulp, but the more expensive grades of paper also contain rags.

17. Although paper is becoming more expensive, it is no longer a luxury item.

EXERCISE 4B

Construct sentences of your own using the helping verbs listed below.

1. can: _____

_____

2. must: _____

_____

3. will: _____

_____

4. should: _____

_____

5. has: _____

_____

6. was: _____

_____

Construct a sentence for each of the following patterns. Make certain that the order of the subjects and verbs in your sentences is the same as the order in the pattern. Use as many different helping and main verbs as possible.

S = subject   HV = helping verb   MV = main verb

7. S - MV: _____

_____

8. S - MV - MV: _____

_____

9. S - HV - MV: _____

_____

10. S - HV - HV - MV: _____

_____

11. S - HV - HV - HV - MV: _____

_____

12. HV - S - MV? _____

_____

(Notice that this pattern produces a question rather than a statement.)

Subject-Verb Identification
Unit Review

Underline the subjects of the following sentences *once* and the verbs *twice*. Some sentences may have more than one subject, more than one verb, or both.

1. Many people suffer from allergies.

2. Allergies can be caused by pollens, food, fur, or even dust.

3. An allergy test can determine the reasons for a person's allergies.

4. In one type of test, small amounts of serum are injected under the patient's skin.

5. Each serum contains a different antigen (an allergy-producing substance).

6. If a person is allergic to a particular antigen, the skin around the site of the injection will swell within a few minutes.

7. The size of the swelling indicates the severity of the allergy.

8. The patient usually receives more than one hundred injections during a three-hour test.

9. The injections are arranged in rows on the patient's upper arms because this part of the body has relatively little sensitivity to pain.

10. By the end of the test, the patient feels like a pincushion and never wants to see another hypodermic needle.

11. Unfortunately, the treatment for allergies consists of still more injections.

12. The patient receives injections several times a week until the body develops an immunity to the antigens in the serum.

13. After several months, the allergies gradually become less severe or may even disappear.

14. However, the injections often continue for years in order to keep the allergies under permanent control.

15. Is the treatment worse than the allergy itself?

16. Everyone with an allergy must eventually make this decision.

Subject-Verb Agreement

5 Recognizing Singular and Plural Subjects and Verbs

Errors in subject-verb agreement are among the most common grammatical mistakes. By applying the rules in this unit, you should be able to correct many of the errors in your own writing.

As you already know, a sentence must contain both a subject and a verb. Read the following two sentences. What is the grammatical difference between them?

The bank opens at ten o'clock in the morning.
The banks open at ten o'clock in the morning.

In the first sentence, the subject *bank* is **singular**. That is, you are talking about only *one* bank. In the second sentence, the subject *banks* is **plural**, meaning that you are talking about *two or more* banks.

Like the subject *bank*, the verb *opens* in the first sentence is **singular**. Verb forms ending in *s* are used with *singular* subjects, as in the sentence "The banker *checks* the vault every day." The verb *open* in the second example is **plural**. This verb form (without a final *s*) is used with *plural* subjects, as in the sentence "The tellers *check* all deposit slips."

In other words, if the subject of a sentence is *singular*, the verb in the sentence must also be *singular*. If the subject of the sentence is *plural*, the verb must be *plural*. This matching of singular subjects with singular verbs and plural subjects with plural verbs is called **subject-verb agreement**.

In order to avoid making mistakes in subject-verb agreement, you must be able to recognize the difference between singular and plural subjects and verbs.

The subjects of sentences are usually nouns or pronouns. As you know, the plurals of nouns are usually formed by adding an *s* to singular forms.

Singular	*Plural*
envelope	envelopes
restaurant	restaurants

However, some nouns have irregular plural forms, such as:

Singular	*Plural*
man	men
child	children
leaf	leaves
medium	media (as in the "mass media")
thesis	theses

Those pronouns which can be used as subjects are also singular or plural, depending upon whether they refer to one or to more than one person or thing.

Singular	*Plural*
I	we
you	you
he, she, it	they

Notice that the pronoun *you* may be either singular or plural.

Although adding an *s* to most nouns makes those nouns plural, adding an *s* to a verb makes the verb *singular*.

Two cooks *prepare* all the meals.
(plural subject and plural verb)
One cook *prepares* all the meals.
(singular subject and singular verb)

An easy way to remember this construction is to memorize the following rule:

Any verb ending in *s* **is** *singular.*

There are no exceptions to this rule. Therefore, it would be incorrect to have a sentence in which a plural subject is matched with a verb ending in *s*.

INCORRECT My parents *lives* in Detroit.
CORRECT My parents *live* in Detroit.
INCORRECT They *has* jobs.
CORRECT They *have* jobs.

(Remember that the principle behind subject-verb agreement is *not* to match subjects that end in *s* with verbs that end in *s* but to match singular subjects, which usually do *not* end in *s*, with singular verbs, which *do* end in *s*. Similarly, plural subjects, which usually *do* end in *s*, are matched with plural verbs, which do *not* end in *s*.)

In order to avoid subject-verb agreement errors, there are a few rules which you should keep in mind. (How you "keep rules in mind" is up to you. If you find that even after you study rules, you still cannot remember them, you should *memorize* the rules in this unit.)

1. A verb agrees with the subject, not with the complement. A complement is a word which refers to the same person or thing as the subject of the sentence. It follows a linking verb.

    Our main economic *problem is* rising prices.

    In the sentence above, the subject is *problem*, which is singular. The subject is not *prices*. Rather, *prices* is the complement. Therefore, the verb takes the singular form *is*. If the sentence is reversed, it now reads:

    Rising *prices are* our main economic problem.

    The subject is now the plural noun *prices* and *problem* is the complement. The verb now takes the plural form *are*. Which are the correct verbs in the following sentences?

    The topic of discussion (was, were) political refugees.
    Astrological signs (seems, seem) to be an interesting subject to many people.

2. Prepositional phrases have no effect on a verb.

> The *President*, with his chief economic advisors, *is having* a press conference today.

In the sentence above, the subject is singular (*President*). The prepositional phrase *with his chief economic advisors* has no effect on the verb, which remains singular (*is having*).

> *One* of the restaurants *serves* authentic Thai food.

The singular verb *serves* agrees with the singular subject *one*, not with the plural object of the preposition (*restaurants*). Which are the correct verbs in the following sentences?

> The woman with her ten cats (was, were) evicted for breaking the clause in her lease which prohibited the keeping of pets.
> The noise of jet airplanes often (keeps, keep) me awake at night.

3. The following **indefinite pronouns** are singular and require singular verbs. (These pronouns are called *indefinite* because they do not refer to a specific person or to a definite thing as do subject pronouns such as *he, she,* or *it.*) These are some common indefinite pronouns, all of which are singular:

> anybody, anyone, anything
>
> each, each one
>
> either, neither
>
> everybody, everyone, everything
>
> nobody, no one, nothing
>
> somebody, someone, something

> *Everybody agrees* with you.
> *Each* of the workers *has* certain responsibilities.
> *Either* of the answers *is* correct.

Notice that in the last two sentences, the verbs agree with the singular subjects *each* and *either*. The verbs are not affected by the plural nouns in the prepositional phrases *of the workers* or *of the answers*.

4. When *each, every,* or *any* is used as an adjective, the subject it modifies requires a *singular* verb.

> *Every* dog and cat *needs* a license.
>
> In some countries, *each* man and woman *carries* a national identity card.

Notice that the adjectives *every* and *each* make the verbs in the sentences singular even though each sentence has more than one subject.

EXERCISE 5A

Circle the verb which correctly completes each sentence. Make certain that you have correctly identified the subject of the sentence and that you have crossed out prepositional phrases.

1. Each of the author's novels (has, have) a similar plot.

2. Chocolate chip cookies (is, are) my favorite dessert.

3. One of the doctors (disagrees, disagree) with the diagnosis made by the other members of the hospital staff.

4. Hot weather with high humidity (makes, make) Washington, D.C., an uncomfortable place to live during the summer.

5. Every television set and radio (was, were) on sale.

6. Neither of the candidates (appeals, appeal) to me.

7. One source of Cecil J. Rhodes' fortune (was, were) diamonds.

8. A suitcase with wheels (enables, enable) me to handle my own luggage.

9 Someone (seems, seem) to be missing from our group.

10. Each museum and art gallery (charges, charge) a small admission fee.

11. The design, along with the quality of the weaving, (helps, help) to determine the price of a Navajo rug.

12. Battered children (is, are) the agency's main concern.

13. Neither of you (has, have) anything to worry about.

14. Every major British playwright and poet (appears, appear) in the anthology.

EXERCISE 5B

Some of the sentences in this exercise contain subject-verb agreement errors. Others are correct as written. If the sentence contains a subject-verb agreement error, cross out the incorrect verb, and write the correct verb in its place. If the sentence is correct, write a *C* in the margin by the sentence number. Be careful not to confuse objects of prepositions with subjects.

1. A major industry in Japan are cultured pearls.

2. The production of pearls occur when an irritant, such as a grain of sand, enters an oyster.

3. To protect its tissue, the oyster coats the irritant with a lustrous substance called nacre.

4. These layers of nacre eventually forms a pearl.

5. In the production of cultured pearls, the irritant is beads made from clam shells.

6. The placement of these beads in oysters are called "seeding."

7. Each of the oysters have to be seeded by hand.

8. In a procedure resembling a surgical operation, a small piece of tissue from another oyster along with a shell bead are placed inside each oyster.

9. Within seven to ten days, cells from the graft tissue begins to surround the bead.

10. The growing period for pearls lasts from one to four years.

11. Longer periods of growth results in larger pearls.

12. The seeding of oysters enable pearls to be mass produced and to be sold at reasonable prices.

6 How Conjunctions and Words Such as <u>There</u> Affect Agreement

Here are additional rules that will help you to determine whether a subject is singular or plural.

5. Two subjects joined by the conjunction *and* are **plural** and require a **plural** verb.

    Los Angeles and *San Francisco* both *lie* on major earthquake faults.

6. Two subjects joined by the conjunctions *or* or *nor* are **singular** and require a **singular** verb.

    Either *soup* or *salad is included* in the price of your dinner.
    Neither the *piano* nor the *organ needs* tuning.

7. If both a singular and a plural subject are joined by *or* or *nor*, the subject which is closer to the verb determines whether the verb is singular or plural.

    Either travelers *checks* or a credit *card is accepted* at this hotel.
    Either a credit *card* or travelers *checks are accepted* at this hotel.

Are travelers checks or a credit *card accepted* at this hotel?
Is a credit card or travelers checks *accepted* at this hotel?

8. In questions and in statements beginning with *there* or *here*, the subject of the sentence *follows* the verb. The words *there* and *here*, as well as interrogatives such as *where, how,* and *when,* are never the subject of the sentence.

   There *are* more than twenty *theaters* in Westwood Village.
   Where *was* your tennis *racket*?
   Here *are* your *tickets* for the concert.
   How *have you been*?

EXERCISE 6A

Circle the verb which correctly completes each sentence.

1. A fool and his money (is, are) soon parted.

2. Either safflower oil or sunflower oil (contains, contain) a high percentage of polyunsaturated fat.

3. The color of jade and its clarity (determines, determine) its value.

4. Neither the pen nor the pencils (belongs, belong) to me.

5. In Hawaii there (is, are) orchids growing wild in people's yards.

6. The violence and vulgarity of this movie (sickens, sicken) me.

7. Why (does, do) ancient Chinese coins have holes in their center?

8. What (is, are) the main ingredients in a New England boiled dinner?

9. Every letter and card (has, have) to meet the post office's minimum size requirements.

10. Either overwork or severe nervous tension (causes, cause) symptoms like yours.

11. Each of the jurors (agrees, agree) that the defendant is guilty.

12. Here (is, are) the set of encyclopedias you wanted.

13. Either carrots or celery (makes, make) a low-calorie snack.

14. One of the tours (includes, include) meals as well as airfare and hotel accommodations.

EXERCISE 6B

Some of the sentences in this exercise contain subject-verb agreement errors. Others are correct as written. If a sentence contains a subject-verb agreement error, cross out the incorrect verb, and write the correct verb in its place. If a sentence is correct, write *C* in the margin by the sentence number.

1. There are a total of twelve animals in the Chinese zodiac system.

2. Each of these animals rule over one lunar year.

3. For example, 1900 and all multiples of 12 after 1900 (1912, 1924, 1948, etc.) are years of the rat.

4. According to Chinese astrological theory, every man and woman born under a particular sign have the personality traits of that animal.

5. For instance, honesty and ambition forms an important part of a rat person's character.

6. Either a dragon person (1940, 1952, 1964) or a monkey person (1944, 1956, 1968) make an ideal mate for a rat person.

7. On the other hand, the marriage of rat people and horse people (1942, 1954, 1966) almost guarantee disaster.

8. A combination of good and bad traits appears in all years.

9. Either stubbornness or short tempers makes ox people (1937, 1949, 1961) difficult to live with.

10. However, cleverness and success are also ox characteristics.

11. The author of this textbook was born in one of the years of the sheep (1931, 1943, 1955).

12. According to her horoscope, wisdom and gentleness abounds in her personality, and she will always have a comfortable life.

13. If you wish to check your own horoscope, many Chinese stores and some public libraries has books describing the Chinese astrological system.

7 Additional Singular and Plural Nouns and Inverted Sentences

The following are some final rules concerning subject-verb agreement.

9. Some words, though plural in form, are singular in meaning and therefore require a **singular** verb.

   > *Physics requires* a prior knowledge of mathematics.
   > *Measles* sometimes *causes* serious complications.

10. A unit of time, weight, or measurement usually requires a **singular** verb because the entire amount is thought of as a single unit.

    > Ten *cents is* the bus fare for senior citizens.
    > 2.2 *pounds equals* one kilogram.

11. Collective nouns usually require **singular** verbs. A **collective noun** is a word which is singular in form but which refers to a group of people or things. Some common collective nouns are words such as *group, team, family, class, crowd,* and *committee.*

    > Our *group meets* at noon on Friday.
    > The *committee raises* money for scholarships.

Occasionally, a collective noun may be used with a plural verb if the writer wishes to show that the members of the group are acting as separate individuals rather than as a unified body. Notice the difference in meaning between the following pairs of sentences.

> The Board of Supervisors *has agreed* to give county workers an 8 percent raise in pay. (In this sentence, the Board is acting as a single, unified group.)
> The Board of Supervisors *are divided* over whether or not to raise taxes. (In this sentence, the Board is viewed as a collection of separate individuals who are not acting as a unified group.)

Because the use of plural verbs with collective nouns occurs very infrequently, when in doubt, it is safer to use a singular verb.

12. Indefinite adjectives and pronouns, such as the words *some, half, all, most,* and *part* may take either singular or plural verbs, depending upon their meaning. If these words tell *how much* of something is meant, the verb is **singular.** If they tell *how many* of something is meant, the verb is **plural.**

> *Most* of the city *is* in ruins. (how much)
> *Most* of the people *are* friendly. (how many)
> *Half* of the steak *is* burnt. (how much)
> *Half* of the guests *have* not *arrived.* (how many)
> *Some* of the food *needs* refrigeration. (how much)
> *Some* of the students *have* the flu. (how many)

(Do not confuse the words in this rule with the words *each, either,* and *neither* in Rule 3. These three words *always* require a *singular* verb.)

13. Some sentences have an inverted pattern in which the verb precedes the subject. Be especially careful to check for subject-verb agreement in this type of sentence.

> In the middle of the park *stands* a *statue* of General Pershing.
> Among his problems *is* a *lack* of money.

Verbs also precede subjects in questions.

Does anyone want something to drink?
Have your *friends* returned yet?

EXERCISE 7A

Circle the verb which correctly completes each sentence.

1. All of the exercises in this unit (deals, deal) with subject-verb agreement.

2. Mumps (makes, make) it difficult for a person to swallow.

3. The Board of Education (has, have) agreed to require all high school students to pass a basic skills test.

4. Eighty dollars a day (is, are) more than I am willing to pay for a hotel room.

5. Some of the cab drivers in Manhattan (seems, seem) to disregard the posted speed limit.

6. Our family (holds, hold) a reunion every summer.

7. Among the paintings in the museum (is, are) a self-portrait by Rembrandt.

8. (Does, Do) each of these cars have a diesel engine?

9. 110 pounds (is, are) the minimum weight for a person donating blood to the Red Cross.

10. A crowd of people usually (gathers, gather) at the scene of an accident.

11. Economics (is, are) required for business majors.

12. Two teaspoons of vanilla extract (provides, provide) the flavoring for this recipe.

13. Most of the houses on this block (needs, need) major repairs.

14. Included with each vacuum cleaner (is, are) attachments for cleaning upholstery and curtains.

15. The team (expects, expect) to have a winning season.

EXERCISE 7B

Some of the sentences in this exercise contain subject-verb agreement errors. Others are correct as written. If a sentence contains a subject-verb agreement error, cross out the incorrect verb, and write the correct form in its place. If the sentence is correct, write *C* in the margin by the sentence number.

1. Among the many breeds of chickens are one called the Araucana.

2. Araucanas differs from other chickens in one major respect: they lay colored eggs.

3. All of the eggs now available in supermarkets come in only two colors—white or brown.

4. However, the colors of Araucana eggs includes pink, blue, and two shades of green.

5. Although hens of other breeds consistently lay eggs of the same color (white or brown), the color of an Araucana's eggs vary within each batch.

6. If an Araucana hen lays one green egg, a blue or pink egg often follow.

7. Nobody knows why Araucanas lay colored eggs.

8. No special feed nor dyes is given to the birds.

9. Except for the color of the shell, there is no differences between Araucana eggs and those of other breeds.

10. Most of the sales of Araucana hens occurs at Easter since Araucanas are advertised in farm journals as "layers of colored Easter eggs."

11. However, no one seem to be selling Araucana eggs commercially.

12. Therefore, it may be years before most of the people in urban areas ever sees an Araucana egg.

Subject-Verb Agreement
Unit Review

Correct any subject-verb agreement errors which you find in the following essay by crossing out the incorrect verb and writing in the correct form. It may help you to underline all the subjects in the essay *once* and all the verbs *twice* before you try to identify errors in agreement.

Although the main purpose of a museum is to display art, a wide range of other functions are performed by New York City's Metropolitan Museum of Art. The size of the museum's facilities and the extent of its collections enables the museum to offer a broad program of cultural activities for the community.

One of the regularly scheduled series of events are the afternoon gallery talks. Each of the talks describe a different portion of the museum's permanent collections. For example, Greek vases is the subject of the gallery talk for November 4th, and Renaissance furnishings and silver is discussed on November 20th. Special gallery talks for children and their parents takes place every Tuesday evening.

In addition to the wide variety of topics covered by the gallery talks, there are also a series of lectures dealing with a single subject, such as famous palaces. The lectures for November and December include descriptions of England's Blenheim Palace (home of the Churchill family) and the Medici Palace (home of the ruling family of Florence during the Italian Renaissance).

The museum also shows several films each week. Most of the films for November and December deals with ancient Greek art.

The gallery talks and films charges no fees. Most of the lectures are also free, but tickets for travelogues cost $4.00. Admission to the museum's classical music concerts range from $4.00 to $7.50.

A senior citizen or museum members does not need to pay to enter the museum. Everyone else are requested to contribute $2.50 or as much as he or she can afford to support the museum's regular exhibits and special programs.

Pronoun Usage

8 Subject, Object, and Possessive Pronouns

Pronouns are words that are used to refer to persons, places, things, and ideas without repeating their names. In other words, pronouns are used in place of nouns. For example, rather than saying "The Coopers bought a new house only last week, but the Coopers have already moved into the house," we can say "The Coopers bought a new house only last week, but *they* have already moved into *it*." In this sentence, the pronoun *they* replaces *Coopers*, and the pronoun *it* replaces *house*. The noun which the pronoun replaces is called the **antecedent** (Latin for "to go before") of the pronoun.

There are several different kinds of pronouns, but in this lesson you will be studying only **subject pronouns, object pronouns,** and **possessive pronouns.**

Singular Pronouns	*Subject*	*Object*	*Possessive*
	I	me	my, mine
	you	you	your, yours
	he	him	his
	she	her	her, hers
	it	it	its

Plural Pronouns	Subject	Object	Possessive
	we	us	our, ours
	you	you	your, yours
	they	them	their, theirs

As their name suggests, **subject pronouns** are used as the *subject* of a sentence or a clause. For example:

She is a design engineer at Hughes Aircraft.
They are graduating from college in June.

In formal speech and writing, subject pronouns are also used after forms of the verb *be*, as in:

That is *he* at the door.
It is *I*.
If I were *she*, I'd take the job.

In formal speech and writing, subject pronouns are used after forms of the verb *be* because they refer to the *same* thing or person as the subject.

That = he at the door.
It = I.
If *I = she*, I'd take the job.

However, in informal speech, many people would use object pronouns in the sentences above.

That is (or *That's*) *him* at the door.
It is (or *It's*) *me*.
If I were *her*, I'd take the job.

Whether you choose to say "it is I" or "it is me" depends upon the circumstances. If you are taking an English test or writing a formal essay, using subject pronouns after forms of *be* is appropriate and expected. But if you are speaking casually with a friend, "it is I" may sound artificial, and the informal "it is me" might be more suitable.

The way in which words and phrases are *actually* used by most people in various situations is called **usage**. In the past, some educated people always used very formal English. Nowadays, however, people are expected to use the type of language which is suitable for a given situation. It is as inappropriate to use very formal language in an informal situation, such as a casual conversation with a close friend, as it is to use informal language, for example slang, in a formal essay.

66

In this unit, you will be studying both grammar and usage. Try to keep clear in your mind those situations in which you have a choice between formal and informal constructions (usage) and those situations in which only one pronoun form is correct at all times (grammar).

"It is *she*" versus "It is *her*" = usage.
"*I* am here" versus "*Me* am here" = grammar.

Object pronouns are used as objects of prepositions, as direct objects, and as indirect objects.

You will remember that the noun or pronoun in a prepositional phrase is called the *object of the preposition*. That is why an *object pronoun* replaces the noun. For example:

Gail drives to work with *Gordon*.
Gail drives to work with *him*.
The professor returned the exams to the *students*.
The professor returned the exams to *them*.

Object pronouns are also used as direct objects. **A direct object** is the word which *receives* the action of the verb, as opposed to the subject, which *performs* the action of the verb.

Frank took the *children* to the park.
(subject)   (direct object)

Frank took *them* to the park.

I have known *Sue* for many years.
(subject)   (direct object)

I have known *her* for many years.

Another way in which object pronouns are used is as indirect objects. An **indirect object** is the person or thing *to whom* or *for whom* something is done.

I lent my *neighbor* a quart of milk.
(subject)   (indirect object) (direct object)

I lent *her* a quart of milk.

(The previous sentence is another way of saying
"I lent a quart of milk *to her*.")

Jean bought her *son* a bicycle.
(subject)   (indirect   (direct
            object)   object)

(The previous sentence is another way of saying
"Jean bought a bicycle *for him.*")

Possessive pronouns are used to show ownership.

The store has *its* summer sale in August.

I left *my* car in the parking lot.

Very few people make pronoun errors when there is only one subject or one object in a sentence. For example, no native speaker of English would say, "Me am here" instead of "I am here." However, people often do make mistakes when two subjects or two objects follow each other in a sentence. For example, which of the following two sentences is grammatically correct?

Mrs. Jones invited my husband and *me* to her party.
Mrs. Jones invited my husband and *I* to her party.

To determine the correct pronoun in this kind of "double" construction, split the sentence in two like this:

1. Mrs. Jones invited my husband to her party.
2. Mrs. Jones invited (me, I) to her party.

As you can tell after you have split the sentence in two, it would be incorrect to say "Mrs. Jones invited *I* to her party." The correct pronoun is *me*, which is the direct object of the verb *invited.* Therefore, the whole sentence should read:

Mrs. Jones invited my husband and *me* to her party.

Which of the following two sentences is correct?

Our supervisor gave Marianne and *I* a promotion.
Our supervisor gave Marianne and *me* a promotion.

Again, split the sentence in two.

1. Our supervisor gave Marianne a promotion.
2. Our supervisor gave (I, me) a promotion.

Now, which pronoun is correct?

Another very common pronoun error is using subject pronouns instead of object pronouns after prepositions. The object of a preposition must be an *object* pronoun. Which of the following two sentences is correct?

> Jerry is going to the party with my sister and *I*.
> Jerry is going to the party with my sister and *me*.

If you split the sentence in two, you have:

1. Jerry is going to the party with my sister.
2. Jerry is going to the party with (I, me).

The correct pronoun is *me*, which is the object of the preposition *with*. Therefore, the correct sentence is:

> Jerry is going to the party with my sister and *me*.

It is extremely important that you do not decide which pronoun to use simply on the basis of what "sounds better" *unless you split the sentence in two first.* To many people, "Mrs. Jones invited my husband and *I* to her party" sounds more "correct" than "Mrs. Jones invited my husband and *me* to her party"; yet, as you have seen, *me* is actually the correct pronoun.

Another example of choosing an incorrect pronoun because it "sounds better" is the frequent misuse of the subject pronoun "I" after the preposition "between." As you already know, the object of a preposition must be an *object* pronoun. Therefore, it is always incorrect to say "between you and *I*." The *correct* construction is "between you and *me*."

Circle the pronoun which correctly completes each of the following sentences.

My cousin and (he, him) are good friends.

The rest of the guests are waiting for you and (I, me).

Are you coming to the airport with your mother and (we, us)?

Can you give Joan and (I, me) a ride home?

I admire (he, him) and you.

Occasionally you may use constructions like the following:

We freshmen must pre-enroll for our classes.
Most of *us nurses* would prefer to work the 7 a.m. to 3 p.m. shift.

To determine whether the sentence requires a subject or an object pronoun, see which pronoun would be correct if the pronoun appeared in the sentence by itself rather than being followed by a noun.

(We, us) actors have a rehearsal tomorrow. =
(We, us) have a rehearsal tomorrow.

Some railroads give a discount to (we, us) students. =
Some railroads give a discount to (we, us).

EXERCISE 8A

The first part of this exercise is intended for a quick review of subject and object pronouns. Reverse each sentence so that the subject pronoun becomes the object and the object pronoun becomes the subject:

Example: *I* waited for *them.*
They waited for *me.*

1. *She* saw *them* every day.

2. *He* helped *you* several times.

3. *I* gave the message to *her.*

4. *We* gave *them* a wedding gift.

5. *He* amused *her* by telling jokes.

6. *They* met *me* at a party.

7. *You* can rely on *us* for help.

8. *I* knew *him* very well.

Circle the pronoun which correctly completes each sentence. Remember to split the sentence if it contains a "double" construction. Apply the rules of formal English usage.

9. You and (she, her) will be working together on this project.

10. The cost of the dinner will be divided between you and (I, me).

11. We and (they, them) are going to a concert tonight.

12. (We, us) truck drivers want lower prices for diesel fuel.

13. Richard and (she, her) have many interests in common.

14. Several guests stayed after the party to help Jim and (I, me) with the dishes.

15. It is (she, her) who needs your help.

16. All of (we, us) flight crew members thank you for flying American Airlines.

17. The Garcias and (we, us) live on the same block.

18. Was it (they, them) who borrowed the keys to my car?

19. What is causing the tension between our company and (they, them)?

20. It was (I, me) who called you last night.

EXERCISE 8B

Some of the following sentences contain pronoun errors. Cross out the incorrect pronouns, and write in the correct forms. If a sentence contains no pronoun errors, label it *C* for *correct*. Apply the rules of formal English usage.

1. Please wait for Ben and I at the airport.

2. The President wants we Americans to conserve energy.

3. Jim and she both have brown belts in judo.

4. Our neighbors and us are having a garage sale this weekend.

5. Are you and he coming to the barbeque?

6. It is me, not you, who need to go on a diet.

7. My youngest sister and me always wore hand-me-downs from our older cousins.

8. Us parents must try to improve the condition of our children's schools.

9. Both him and his wife plan to become architects.

10. If I were him, I'd try to get a better job.

11. Would you like to go to the beach with my children and me?

12. All of we who live on this block should demand that the city install brighter street lights.

13. It will be easier for her and I to fly to San Francisco rather than to drive.

14. The combination to the safe is known only to the president of the bank and her.

15. This information must be kept a secret between you and I.

9 Pronouns in Comparisons and Pronouns with -self, -selves

Using Pronouns in Comparisons

In speech and in writing, we often compare two people or two things with each other. For example:

Rose is older than *I* am.
The company pays *Ellen* a higher salary than it pays *me*.

In the sentences above, it is easy to tell whether a subject pronoun or an object pronoun should be used in each comparison. In the first sentence, the subject pronoun *I* is correct because it would be clearly ungrammatical to say that "Rose is older than *me* am." In the second sentence, the object pronoun *me* is correct because you would not say that "The company pays Ellen a higher salary than it pays *I*."

However, people usually do not write out their comparisons completely. They use a shortened form instead. For example:

Mary Anne plays tennis better than *I*.
The accident injured *Sam* more than *me*.

In these cases, it is possible to determine which pronoun is correct by mentally filling in the words which have been left out of the comparison.

Mary Anne plays tennis better than I (do).
The accident injured Sam more than (it injured) me.

Fill in the missing words to determine which pronouns are correct in the following sentences.

Clarence can run longer distances than (I, me).

I enjoy classical music more than (he, him).

This trip will be more interesting for you than (she, her).

When you fill in the missing words, the correct comparisons are:

Clarence can run longer distances than I (can).
I enjoy classical music more than he (does).
This trip will be more interesting for you than (it will be for) her.

In *informal* usage, you often hear people use object pronouns instead of subject pronouns in comparisons. (For example, "He's taller than me" instead of "He's taller than I.") However, these forms are generally considered inappropriate in writing and formal speech. You should be especially careful in situations where the wrong pronoun can change the meaning of the entire sentence. For example, "Mary danced with George more than *I* (danced with him)" does not mean the same thing as "Mary danced with George more than (she danced with) *me*." In addition, using the wrong pronoun can sometimes lead to unintentionally ridiculous sentences, such as:

My girlfriend likes pizza more than me.

Unless your girlfriend happens to like food more than she likes you, the correct pronoun would be:

My girlfriend likes pizza more than *I* (do).

(Note: The conjunction *than*, which is used in comparisons, should not be confused with the adverb *then*.)

Avoiding Doubled Subjects

Do not "double," or repeat, the subject of a sentence by repeating the noun in its pronoun form.

INCORRECT My mother, she works at Kaiser Hospital.
CORRECT My mother works at Kaiser Hospital.
INCORRECT The Rams, they moved from Los Angeles to Anaheim.
CORRECT The Rams moved from Los Angeles to Anaheim.

Pronouns with –self, –selves

Some pronouns end in *–self* or *–selves*:

Singular	*Plural*
myself	ourselves
yourself	yourselves
himself	themselves
herself	
itself	

These pronouns can be used in two ways. They can be **reflexive pronouns**, which are used when the object of the verb or of the preposition is the same person as the subject. For example:

I hurt *myself.* (I = myself)
She did the work by *herself.* (she = herself)

Or they may be used for *emphasis.*

The prisoner *himself* confessed to the crime.
I painted my entire apartment *myself.*

Notice that the singular forms of reflexive pronouns end in *self*, and the plural forms end in *selves*. In standard English, there are no such forms as *hisself, ourselfs, theirselfs,* or *themselfs.* These forms are considered non-standard in both speech and writing and should be avoided unless you are using a dialect in which they are the customary forms.

In formal English, the reflexive pronoun *myself* is not used in place of a subject or object pronoun.

INCORRECT	Lauren and *myself* would like to have dinner with you.
CORRECT	Lauren and *I* would like to have dinner with *you*.
INCORRECT	A friend is teaching Cathy and *myself* how to play badminton.
CORRECT	A friend is teaching Cathy and *me* how to play badminton.

Myself is sometimes used as a subject or object in informal usage, but even in these cases the use of the correct subject or object pronoun is preferred. Referring to yourself as *myself* rather than as *I* or *me* does *not* make you sound more polite or more modest.

EXERCISE 9A

Circle the pronoun which most logically and correctly completes each sentence. Apply the rules of formal English usage.

1. Although we both drive the same kind of car, I get better mileage than (he, him).

2. Jane asked my sister and (I, me) to be her bridesmaids.

3. They always insist on doing everything (themselfs, themselves).

4. She enjoyed the movie more than (he, him).

5. I'm sure that you and (she, her) will enjoy your vacation in Canada.

6. Either Juan or (I, myself) will take you to the doctor.

7. We're both full-time students, but you seem to have more free time than (I, me).

8. The bus strike affects you more than (they, them) since you have no car.

9. That color suits you better than (he, him).

10. Since we all had the same food for lunch, why did the waitress charge Bob more than (we, us)?

11. Despite the television commercials for detergents, I really don't care if you have whiter laundry than (I, me).

12. Please leave the keys with either my neighbor or (me, myself).

13. If the decision were up to (we, us) employees, our lunch break would be a full hour instead of forty-five minutes.

14. The stewardess forgot to serve dinner to the passengers in the next row and (we, us).

15. We will probably arrive at the party earlier than (they, them).

EXERCISE 9B

If a sentence contains a pronoun error, cross out the incorrect pronoun, and write in the correct form. If a sentence has a "doubled subject," correct this mistake. If a sentence contains no pronoun errors, label it *C* for *correct*. Apply the rules of formal English usage.

1. He is a much better cook than her.

2. The lawyers reminded we jury members that the defendant's guilt must be proven beyond a reasonable doubt.

3. Despite their language problems, many foreign students seem to do better in science classes than us Americans.

4. Since the other driver did not have the right of way, he is more responsible for the accident than us.

5. Although my niece is younger and smaller than my nephew, she gets into twice as much mischief as he.

6. While trying to catch a Frisbee, John and I ran into each other, and the collision knocked both him and I to the ground.

7. Would you like to go roller skating with Amy and I this afternoon?

8. Do you or him know the way to San Jose?

9. These politicians, they don't seem to know what they're doing.

10. They will hurt themselfs if they're not careful.

11. Did you know that Portia and myself live only two blocks from your house?

12. They are not as good tennis doubles partners as you and me.

13. It's difficult to know whether us or our children enjoy the county fair more.

14. Was it them who kept playing their stereo till two in the morning?

15. Astronomy interests Wayne more than me.

10 Agreement of Pronouns with Their Antecedents

Agreement in Number

Like nouns, pronouns may be either singular or plural, depending upon whether they refer to one or to more than one person or thing. Following are the subject, object, and possessive pronouns you have learned, divided into singular and plural categories.

Singular Pronouns	*Subject*	*Object*	*Possessive*
	I	me	my, mine
	you	you	your, yours
	he	him	his
	she	her	her, hers
	it	it	its

Plural Pronouns	*Subject*	*Object*	*Possessive*
	we	us	our, ours
	you	you	your, yours
	they	them	their, theirs

Just as a subject must agree in number with its verb, a pronoun must agree in number with its **antecedent.** (The antecedent, you will remember, is the noun to which the pronoun refers.) In other words, if the antecedent is *singular*, the pronoun must be *singular*. If the antecedent is *plural*, the pronoun must be *plural*.

Study the following sentences, in which both the pronouns and their antecedents have been italicized.

Because the *car* wouldn't start, *it* was towed to the nearest gas station. Because the *cars* had a serious mechanical defect, *they* were recalled by the manufacturer.

Obviously, few people would make pronoun agreement errors in the above sentences since *car* is clearly singular, and *cars* is clearly plural. However, people often make pronoun agreement errors in cases like the following:

INCORRECT If an airline *passenger* wants to be certain not to miss *their* flight, *they* should arrive at the airport an hour before the scheduled departure time.

CORRECT If an airline *passenger* wants to be certain not to miss *his* flight, *he* should arrive at the airport an hour before the scheduled departure time.

INCORRECT Every working *person* must have *their* own Social Security card.

CORRECT Every working *person* must have *his* own Social Security card.

What causes people to make mistakes like these? The mistakes probably occur because when the writer describes a *passenger*, he or she is thinking of passengers in general. Similarly, the writer may think of a *person* as people in general. Nevertheless, since *passenger* and *person* are singular nouns, they must be used with singular pronouns. Notice that if several pronouns all refer to the same antecedent, *all* of the pronouns must agree in number with the antecedent.

Wendy plans to spend *her* summer in France because *she* is a French major.
Whenever my neighbors go on a vacation, *they* take both of *their* cats with *them.*

Another common pronoun agreement error involves *indefinite pronouns.* As you learned in the unit on subject-verb agreement (on page 42), indefinite pronouns are *singular* and require *singular* verbs. (For example, "Everyone *is* here," *not* "Everyone *are* here.") Similarly, when indefinite pronouns are used as antecedents, they require *singular* subject and object pronouns.

The following words are singular indefinite pronouns:

> anybody, anyone, anything
>
> each, each one
>
> either, neither
>
> everybody, everyone, everything
>
> nobody, no one, nothing
>
> somebody, someone, something

Notice the use of singular pronouns with these words.

Everyone did as *he* pleased.
Somebody has forgotten *her* purse.
Either of the choices has *its* disadvantages.

In informal spoken English, plural pronouns are often used with indefinite pronoun antecedents. However, this construction is generally not considered appropriate in formal speech or writing.

INFORMAL   *Somebody* should let you borrow *their* book.
FORMAL   *Somebody* should let you borrow *his* book.

In some sentences, an indefinite pronoun is so clearly plural in meaning that a singular pronoun sounds awkward with it. For example:

Everyone on this block must be wealthy because *he* drives a Cadillac or a Continental.

In cases such as this, the sentence should be reworded.

All the *people* on this block must be wealthy because *they* all drive a Cadillac or a Continental.

Although the matching of singular pronouns with singular antecedents is a *grammatical* problem, a *usage* problem may occur if the pronoun's antecedent refers to both sexes. In the past, singular masculine pronouns were used to refer to singular antecedents, such as "person" or "passenger," even if these antecedents included women as well as men. Now, with the increased emphasis on the status of women in society, some writers prefer to use alternate forms, such as *he or she* or *his or her*, as in the sentence beginning "The mistakes probably occur . . ." on page 84.

> Every *student* must make certain that *he or she* registers as early as possible.
> *Everyone* must do *his or her* best to conserve energy.

Since this is a question of usage, not of grammar, the decision of which construction to use is your own. However, in order to simplify the rules for you while you are still studying grammar, the exercises in this unit will offer you the choice between only one singular pronoun (either masculine or feminine) and one plural pronoun. For example:

> Each supervisor is responsible for the performance of (her, their) employees.
> Everyone should mind (his, their) own business.

Which pronouns would be correct in the following sentences according to the rules of formal English usage?

> Neither of the professors had (her, their) office hours at a time that was convenient for me.
> If a coach wants to have a winning team, (he, they) must recruit promising new players.
> Someone has forgotten to turn off (his, their) car's lights.
> Each of the women said that (she, they) had benefited from taking a course in self-defense.

Agreement in Person

In grammar, pronouns are classified into groups called **persons. First person** refers to the person who is speaking. **Second person** is the person being spoken to. **Third person** is the person or thing being spoken about. Below is a chart of subject pronouns grouped according to person.

	Singular	*Plural*
first person	I	we
second person	you	you
third person	he, she, it	they

All nouns are considered third person (either singular or plural) because nouns can be replaced by third-person pronouns (for example, *Bob = he*; *a book = it*; *apples = they*).

Just as a pronoun and its antecedent must agree in number, they must also agree in person. Agreement in person usually becomes a problem only when the second-person pronoun *you* is incorrectly used with a third-person antecedent. Study the following examples.

INCORRECT If *anyone* wants to vote, *you* must register first.

CORRECT If *anyone* wants to vote, *he* must register first.

INCORRECT When *drivers* get caught in a traffic jam, *you* become impatient.

CORRECT When *drivers* get caught in a traffic jam, *they* become impatient.

This type of mistake is called a **shift in person** and is considered a serious grammatical error.

In addition to avoiding shifts in person within individual sentences, you should also try to be consistent in your use of person when you are writing essays. In general, an entire essay is written in the same person. If, for example, you are writing an essay about the special problems faced by students who work full-time, you will probably use either the first or the third person. You should avoid shifts into the second person (*you*) since *you* refers to the reader of your paper and not to the students you are writing about.

INCORRECT *Students* who work full-time often find it difficult to study. For example, *you* often come home from *your* job too exhausted to concentrate on *your* homework.

CORRECT *Students* who work full-time often find it difficult to study. For example, *they* often come home from *their* job too exhausted to concentrate on *their* homework.

EXERCISE 10A

Circle the pronoun which correctly completes each sentence. Apply the rules of formal English usage.

1. Everyone here is free to express (her, their) own opinion.

2. Either Jeffrey or Brian will lend you (his, their) slide projector.

3. If a person wants to get a driver's license, (she, they) must pass a written test, a driving test, and an eye exam.

4. Many people have difficulty managing (his, their) money during times of inflation.

5. Before anyone travels overseas, (he, you) should obtain a passport.

6. Each applicant for a passport must submit two photographs of (herself, themselves) and pay a fee of thirteen dollars.

7. A runner training for a marathon must build up both (his, their) endurance and speed.

8. No one can succeed in life if (he, you) lacks persistence.

9. Neither of the apartment buildings had (its, their) own swimming pool.

10. Although Jerry and (he, him) disagree about politics, economics, and religion, they are still good friends.

11. Your news came as a complete surprise to my friends and (I, me).

12. I have been waiting in line much longer than (they, them).

13. In some states, a teacher must be fingerprinted before (he, they) can be issued a credential.

14. The state prison in Walla Walla, Washington, is, to a large extent, run by the prisoners (theirselves, themselves).

15. If someone has a suggestion, (she, they) should speak up now.

EXERCISE 10B

If a sentence contains an error in pronoun usage, cross out the incorrect pronoun, and write in the correct form. Some sentences may contain more than one error. If a sentence contains no pronoun errors, label it *C* for *correct*. Apply the rules of formal English usage.

1. Does somebody have a dime they can lend me?

2. New York's JFK International Airport needs to make their ticketing and check-in procedures more efficient.

3. If everyone chooses their goals realistically, they will have a better chance of succeeding.

4. Most visitors to Los Angeles rent a car because it is difficult for you to get around the city without an automobile.

5. Whenever I buy a carton of milk, I check its pull date to make certain that the milk is fresh.

6. Visitors to New York City will find that you really don't need a car.

7. No one remembered to bring their guitar to the picnic.

8. They watch a lot more television than us.

9. I didn't know that you and her were planning to get married.

10. Anyone who suffers from motion sickness can take a Dramamine tablet half an hour before their trip begins.

11. Would you like to come to Sea World with my family and I?

12. We bought a large pizza and divided it between they and we.

13. Your smoking is bothering Judy and me.

14. The insurance salesman tried to sell my husband and myself a policy.

15. I deserve the promotion because I have more experience than him.

11 Order of Pronouns and Spelling of Possessives

Order of Pronouns

When you are referring to someone else and to yourself in the same sentence, mention the other person's name (or the pronoun which replaces the name) before you mention your own.

INCORRECT *I* and *Jean* work in the same studio.

CORRECT *Jean* and *I* work in the same studio.

INCORRECT Please give your application to *me* or *him.*

CORRECT Please give your application to *him* or *me.*

This construction is actually not a rule of grammar; rather, it is considered a matter of courtesy.

Possessive Pronouns

Here is a list of possessive pronouns which you have already studied. This time, look carefully at how they are spelled and punctuated.

	Singular	*Plural*
first person	my, mine	our, ours
second person	your, yours	your, yours
third person	his	their, theirs
	her, hers	
	its	

Possessive pronouns do *not* contain apostrophes.

    INCORRECT The skis are *her's.*
      CORRECT The skis are *hers.*

Be especially careful not to confuse the possessive pronoun *its* with the contraction *it's* (it is).

    INCORRECT The newspaper is not being published because *it's* printers are on strike.
      CORRECT The newspaper is not being published because *its* printers are on strike.

Also, do not confuse the following pairs of words: *whose*, which is the possessive form of *who*, with *who's* (who is); *your*, which is the possessive form of *you*, with *you're* (you are); and *their*, which is the possessive form of *they*, with *they're* (they are).

I don't know *whose* car that is.
I don't know *who's* going to teach the class.
Your suitcase is unlocked.
You're an excellent mechanic.
Have you bought any of *their* paintings?
They're both professional artists.

A final note: When you do pronoun exercises, or when you use pronouns in your own writing, remember to apply the rules. If you rely only on what "sounds right," your ear will usually supply only those pronouns which are appropriate in *informal* English.

EXERCISE 11A

If a sentence contains an error in pronoun usage, cross out the incorrect pronoun, and write in the correct form. Some sentences may contain more than one error. If a sentence contains no pronoun errors, label it *C* for *correct*. Apply the rules of formal English usage.

1. This gift is from me and Alan.

2. Its possible that your car may need to have its transmission replaced.

3. Who's dog is running through our yard?

4. These papers aren't mine, so they must be your's.

5. Whose coming to the party besides us?

6. Their going to redecorate they're home.

7. If you have any questions about fossils, ask I or Natalie.

8. Your moving to Seattle next week, aren't you?

9. If you want to borrow my pick-up truck, it's all right with me.

10. An English sheepdog makes a good watchdog for a family with small children because although its very large, its not vicious.

11. Us bank tellers know how boring it is to handle money all day long.

12. Please call a cab for Joe and I.

EXERCISE 11B

If a sentence contains an error in pronoun usage, cross out the incorrect pronoun, and write in the correct form. Some sentences may contain more than one error. If a sentence contains no pronoun errors, label it *C* for *correct*. Apply the rules of formal English usage.

1. I and my brother are planning a surprise party for our parents' twenty-fifth anniversary.

2. Buffalo, New York, has its attractions, but it's winter weather isn't one of them.

3. Some companies paint their office walls yellow on the theory that a cheerful color will make they're employees more efficient.

4. Whose the person who's car is blocking our driveway?

5. If anyone hasn't received their paycheck, they should notify the payroll office immediately.

6. If a person wants to see movie stars or other celebrities, you should shop on Rodeo Drive in Beverly Hills, California.

7. Karen and I used to jog together every morning, but now she can run faster than me.

8. The typist produced a clearer-looking page because they used a carbon film rather than a nylon ribbon.

9. Is this sweater his or your's?

10. My daughter looks more like her father than me.

11. Pregnant women should not take unnecessary medication, or you may endanger your child's development.

12. The argument is between he and Virginia, and the rest of us should not get ourselfs involved.

Pronoun Usage
Unit Review

Part One   Some of the following sentences contain pronoun errors. Cross out the incorrect pronouns, and write in the correct forms. If a sentence contains no pronoun errors, label it *C* for *correct*. Apply the rules of formal English.

1. The border patrol asked my friend and I for our passports.

2. If anyone wants to study kung fu, you should have good coordination and quick reflexes.

3. The pilot asked we passengers to remain in our seats until the plane came to a complete stop.

4. Are you as determined to stop smoking as I?

5. The outlaw threatened to shoot they and us unless the sheriff dropped his guns.

6. When your in Rome, do as the Romans do.

7. No one is allowed to bring their dog into this store.

8. I accidentally spilled some coffee on Sally and he.

9. Either Elaine or myself will represent our company at the convention.

10. Who's umbrella is that?

11. They designed and built their home themselfs.

12. It's difficult to give a dinner party nowadays because everyone seems to be on their own special diet.

Part Two   Correct any pronoun errors which you find in the following letter. Apply the rules of formal English usage.

Dear Mr. Greene:

This note is to explain why I have been absent from you're class this week.

My husband he was hurt in a construction accident at work. Part of a scaffold collapsed and let he and another man fall from the third floor to the ground. My husband has been in this hospital since Monday with three fractured vertebrae. The other man was hurt even worse than him.

Going to the hospital every day has left me way behind in my own work. My two oldest children they try to help out, but their only eight and ten years old and can't do all the housework their-selves. Its all they can do to take care of the other two children. Next week, though, my sister is coming to stay with my family and I to help us out, so I think I'll be able to return to school then.

I hope that you can sympathize with the problems myself and my family are having and will let me make up the work I have missed.

Sincerely,
Annie Malone

Compound and Complex Sentences Versus Run-On Sentences and Fragments

12 Compound Sentences

A **compound sentence**, as you learned in Lesson 2 (see page 12), contains *at least two subjects and two verbs*, usually arranged in an S-V/S-V pattern. For example:

S   V   S   V

Our old car used too much gas, so we bought a more economical model.

S V   S   V

The restaurant's food is excellent, and its prices are reasonable.

In grammar, the term *compound* means "having two or more parts." Thus, the sentence "*Lemons, limes,* and *kumquats* are all citrus fruits" has a **compound subject.** "The tanker truck *overturned* and *blocked* three lanes of the freeway" has a **compound verb.**

A compound sentence can be divided into two parts, each of which can be a separate sentence by itself.

Our old car used too much gas.

+

We bought a more economical model.

The restaurant's food is excellent.

$$+$$

Its prices are reasonable.

Since a compound sentence can be divided into *two* separate sentences, each half of a compound sentence must contain at least one subject and one verb. Therefore, each half of a compound sentence is a **clause**. A clause is a group of words which contains both a subject and a verb. (In contrast, a group of words which does not contain both a subject and a verb is called a **phrase**, as in a prepositional phrase.) A clause which can stand alone as a complete sentence is called an **independent clause**. Since each clause in a compound sentence can stand alone as a complete sentence, each clause must be independent. In other words:

A compound sentence consists of at least two independent clauses joined together to form a single sentence.

There are two ways to join independent clauses in order to form a compound sentence. The most frequently used method is to put a conjunction between the clauses. A **conjunction** is a word that joins words or groups of words. In grammar, *coordinate* means "of equal importance." The conjunctions which are used in compound sentences are called **coordinate conjunctions** because they join two groups of words which are of equal grammatical importance (they are both independent clauses). The following coordinate conjunctions are used to join the clauses of compound sentences:

> and
>
> but
>
> for (when used as a synonym for "because" rather
>   than as a preposition)
>
> nor
>
> or
>
> so
>
> yet

You should *memorize* these coordinate conjunctions because later you will have to be able to distinguish between them and the conjunctions which are used to form complex sentences (page 112).

In the following sentences, underline the subjects of the compound sentences *once* and the verbs *twice*, and circle the coordinate conjunction which joins the clauses. Notice that a comma precedes the coordinate conjunction.

The auditorium's lights dimmed, and the orchestra began to play.

My supermarket always has contests, but I never win any prizes.

We rarely watch television during the summer, for most of the programs are re-runs.

You should do warm-up exercises before jogging, or you may strain your muscles.

She doesn't speak English, nor does her husband.

Tomorrow is a legal holiday, so the banks will be closed.

I have met that man before, yet I can't remember his name.

Construct compound sentences of your own, using the coordinate conjunctions listed below to join your clauses. Underline the subject of each clause *once* and the verb *twice*. (You may construct a clause that has more than one subject and/or more than one verb, but each clause must have *at least* one subject and one verb.)

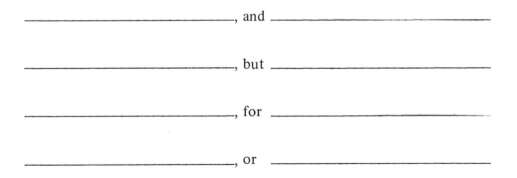

The second way to join the clauses in a compound sentence is to use a semicolon (;) *in place of both the comma and the coordinate conjunction.* For example:

I don't have my wallet; I must have left it at home.
Summers in Los Angeles are warm and dry; it rarely rains between June and September.

Compound sentences constructed with semicolons occur less frequently than compound sentences constructed with coordinate conjunctions because a conjunction is usually needed to show the relationship between the clauses. For example, without a coordinate conjunction the logical relationship between the two clauses in the following sentence might be confusing.

The cashier charged me $25.00; the bill was incorrect.

If, however, you replace the semicolon with a coordinate conjunction, the relationship between the clauses becomes clear.

The cashier charged me $25.00, *but* the bill was incorrect.

Therefore, when you construct compound sentences of your own, use semicolons only when the relationship between the clauses is clear even without the use of a coordinate conjunction.

Construct two compound sentences of your own, using semicolons to join the clauses. Underline the subjects *once* and the verbs *twice*. Make certain that each clause has at least one subject and one verb.

_____; _____

_____; _____

As you can see from the sentences which you have constructed, the following punctuation rules apply to compound sentences:

1. If the clauses in a compound sentence are joined by a coordinate conjunction, place a comma before (to the left of) the conjunction.

   This sentence is compound, and it contains a comma.

   You may have learned that it is not necessary to use commas in short compound sentences (for example, "He's a Scorpio and I'm a Libra"). Although this is true, not everyone agrees on how short a "short" compound sentence is, so if you are in doubt, it is safer to use a comma. All the sentences in the exercises for this unit will be "long" compound sentences and should have a comma before the conjunction.

2. Although a compound sentence may contain more than one con-

junction, the comma is placed only before the conjunction which joins the clauses.

> My aunt *and* uncle are arriving on the two o'clock plane, *and* I must meet them at the airport.

3. If the clauses in a compound sentence are *not* joined by a coordinate conjunction, place a semicolon between the clauses.

> The bride wore an antique lace veil; it had once belonged to her great-grandmother.

The following sentence patterns do *not* require commas because they are **simple** (meaning that they contain only one clause) rather than compound.

S-V-V: She slipped on the icy sidewalk and twisted her ankle. (no comma)

S-S-V: Fry bread and mutton stew are staples of the traditional Navajo diet. (no comma)

S-S-V-V: My children and I went to the beach and built castles in the sand. (no comma)

To review, the two patterns for punctuating a compound sentence are:

clause + comma + coordinate conjunction + clause
I live near the ocean, so I often go to the beach.

clause + semicolon + clause
I can't eat dessert; I'm on a diet.

EXERCISE 12A

Make each of the following independent clauses a compound sentence by adding an appropriate coordinate conjunction and a second independent clause. Try to use as many different conjunctions in this exercise as possible. Remember to place a comma before the coordinate conjunction.

1. It was 95 degrees yesterday _____

   _____

2. He tried to think of a topic for his essay _____

   _____

3. I'm not feeling well _____

   _____

4. You must pay the fine _____

   _____

5. All the stores were closed _____

   _____

Write compound sentences of your own, using the coordinate conjunctions listed below. Remember to place a comma before the coordinate conjunction which divides the clauses, and make certain that each of your clauses contains at least one subject and one verb.

6. and: _____

   _____

7. but: _____

_____

8. for: _____

_____

9. or: _____

_____

10. nor: _____

_____

11. so: _____

_____

12. yet: _____

_____

Construct two compound sentences of your own, punctuated with semi-colons.

13. _____

_____

14. _____

_____

EXERCISE 12B

Add commas and semicolons to the following sentences wherever they are needed. If a sentence needs no additional punctuation (in other words, if the sentence is simple rather than compound), label it *C* for *correct*.

1. Look at an Asian painting and you may see a small red seal stamped in one of its corners.

2. This seal bears the artist's name and is called a "chop."

3. Chops are not confined to paintings they can be used on any document requiring an official signature in some Asian countries.

4. For example, a chop may be stamped on a contract the red seal is as legally valid as a handwritten signature.

5. Chops are carved out of stone or other hard materials.

6. Ordinary chops are often made of granite but more expensive chops of jade or other precious stones are also available.

7. The owner's name is hand-carved into the base of the chop in Chinese characters the characters must be carved backwards in order to produce a positive impression.

8. Chops are very difficult to forge for their hand-carving makes each of them an individual work of art.

9. A chop is used like a rubber stamp it is pressed against an ink pad and then stamped on paper.

10. The ink used for chops is bright red and has the texture of canned shoe polish.

11. In the United States chops have no legal status so they are often used for decorative purposes.

12. For example, I use my chop to stamp my name in books and to personalize my stationery.

13 Complex Sentences

There are two kinds of clauses, independent and dependent. As you have seen, **independent clauses** can stand alone as complete sentences. For example:

I drive a Volkswagen Rabbit.
Judy is the youngest of seven children.

A **dependent clause**, however, *cannot* stand alone as a complete sentence. Instead, it must be attached to, or *depend* upon, an *independent* clause in order to form a grammatically complete sentence and to express a complete idea. Notice that the following dependent clauses are *not* complete sentences.

Whenever I have the time . . .
If you have any extra money . . .
Because Rob hopes to become an actor . . .

These clauses seem incomplete because they are actually only *half* of a sentence. Using the first of the following sentences as a model, change each dependent clause into a complete sentence by adding an appropriate *independent* clause.

Whenever I have the time, *I play racketball.*

_____

If you have any extra money, _____

_____

Because Rob hopes to become an actor, _____

_____

You have now constructed two complex sentences. A **complex sentence** contains both independent and dependent clauses. (In contrast, a **compound sentence** contains only *independent* clauses.)

Every dependent clause begins with a subordinate conjunction. You will recall that a **conjunction** is a word that joins words or groups of words. The conjunctions which begin dependent clauses are called **subordinate conjunctions** because the word *subordinate* means "of lesser importance." Grammatically speaking, a dependent clause is "less important" than an independent clause because it cannot stand alone as a complete sentence. (The conjunctions which are used to form compound sentences are called **coordinate conjunctions** because *coordinate* means "of equal importance." Since both of the clauses in a compound sentence are independent, both clauses are "of equal importance.")

The type of dependent clause which you will be studying in this lesson is called an **adverb clause** because, like an adverb, an adverb clause describes a verb (or sometimes an adjective or an adverb). It is the same kind of clause which you worked with in Lesson 2, pages 13–14. The subordinate conjunctions used to begin adverb clauses describe verbs by telling *how, when, where, why,* or *under what conditions* the action occurs.

how: as if, as though

when: after, as, as soon as, before, until, when, whenever, while

where: where, wherever

why: because, in order that, since, so that

under what conditions: although, as long as, even though, if, though, unless

Read the following sentences. A slanted line indicates the point at which each sentence divides into two separate clauses. Underline the subject of each clause *once* and the verb *twice*. Circle the subordinate conjunction.

When dinner is ready, / I'll call you.

Because he works at nights and on weekends, / he doesn't have much time for a social life.

We'll go to the beach / after the fog lifts.

Now examine the clause in each sentence which contains the circled subordinate conjunction.

The clause which contains the subordinate conjunction is the dependent clause.

Notice that in a complex sentence, the dependent clause may be either the first or the second clause in the sentence.

If you are not feeling well, you should stay home.
Your car runs very well *even though it's ten years old.*

In most cases, the adverb clauses in a complex sentence are *reversible*. That is, the sentence has the same basic meaning no matter which clause comes first. For example:

If it rains, the baseball game will be postponed.

or

The baseball game will be postponed *if it rains*.

I can't go to Europe *until I save some more money.*

or

Until I save some more money, *I can't go to Europe.*

However, the order of the clauses in a complex sentence does affect the punctuation of the sentence.

1. If the **dependent** clause is the first clause in the sentence, it is followed by a comma.

   While you are on vacation, I'll take care of your mail.

2. If the **independent** clause is the first clause in the sentence, no comma is needed.

> I'll take care of your mail *while you are on vacation.* (no comma)

Punctuate the following complex sentences. First circle the subordinate conjunction in each sentence, and draw a slanted line between the clauses.

After we eat dinner we're going to see a movie.

The child carries her teddy bear with her wherever she goes.

If it doesn't rain the crops will be ruined.

As soon as I finish painting my apartment I'll help you paint yours.

EXERCISE 13A

Complete each of the following complex sentences by adding an appropriate adverb clause (one that makes sense in the sentence). Add commas where they are necessary.

1. The movie was a success because _____

_____

2. If _____

the team can win its next game.

3. When _____

we'll move to a larger apartment.

4. The plane will take off as soon as _____

_____

5. Although _____

we still enjoyed the party.

Construct complex sentences of your own, using the following subordinate conjunctions to form your adverb clauses. Add commas where they are necessary.

6. _____ _____ since

_____

7. Until _____

_____

8. While _____

_____

9. _____ unless

_____

10. _____ so that

_____

EXERCISE 13B

First underline the dependent clauses in the following complex sentences. Then add commas to the sentences if they are necessary. If a sentence needs no additional punctuation, label it *C* for *correct*.

1. When I visited Amsterdam in 1975 I had an unusual and memorable experience.

2. While I was walking through one of the city's most expensive shopping areas I suddenly began to hiccup very loudly.

3. I was embarrassed because other pedestrians were staring at me.

4. I decided to go into a store so that I could get a drink of water.

5. Although at the time I was unaware of the fact almost no European stores have public drinking fountains.

6. As I entered the store I noticed that it had shelves full of beautiful china and glassware.

7. I wandered through the store looking for a drinking fountain until a saleswoman approached me.

8. I asked her if I could please have a drink of water.

9. While I watched in surprise she walked to the nearest shelf and picked up a tall crystal goblet.

10. I followed her through the store until we came to a tiny back room with a small sink.

11. The saleswoman carefully rinsed the glass before she filled it with water and gave it to me.

12. As I was drinking the water I noticed a price tag on the bottom of the glass.

13. Since the price was marked in Dutch guilders it took me a minute to calculate the equivalent amount in American dollars.

14. I began to choke as I realized the price of the goblet—fifty-five dollars.

15. Because I was so shocked at the idea of drinking from a fifty-five dollar glass my hiccups suddenly stopped.

16. The saleswoman rinsed and wiped the glass and replaced it on the shelf so that it looked brand new.

17. She told me to be sure to visit the store again if I ever returned to Amsterdam.

18. Whenever I think of Amsterdam I remember my fifty-five dollar glass of water and the kindness of the Dutch people.

14 Avoiding Run-On Sentences and Comma Splices

As you learned in Lesson 12 (see page 102), a compound sentence consists of at least two independent clauses. The independent clauses in a compound sentence must be separated either by a coordinate conjunction (such as *and, but, or*) preceded by a comma or by a semicolon if no conjunction is used.

Failure to separate two independent clauses results in an error known as a **run-on sentence**. The following are examples of run-on sentences.

I don't play tennis well I have a poor backhand.
The 1984 Olympics will be held in Los Angeles many of the city's residents do not want to have the games there.

Run-on sentences are very serious errors. They are not only confusing to the reader, but they also indicate that the writer cannot tell where one sentence ends and another begins.

There are three ways to correct a run-on sentence.

1. Divide the run-on into two separate sentences, ending each sentence with a period. (If the sentences are questions, end them with question marks.)

I don't play tennis well. I have a poor backhand.

The 1984 Olympics will be held in Los Angeles. Many of the city's residents do not want to have the games there.

Although this method produces grammatically correct sentences, an essay written completely in short simple sentences creates the choppy effect of an elementary school reading text. Therefore, you should also consider using the two other methods of correcting run-ons.

2. Change the run-on to a **compound sentence** by separating the clauses with a semicolon or with a coordinate conjunction preceded by a comma.

I don't play tennis well; I have a poor backhand.

The 1984 Olympics will be held in Los Angeles, *but* many of city's residents do not want to have the games there.

3. Change the run-on to a **complex sentence** by placing a subordinate conjunction between the clauses.

I don't play tennis well *because* I have a poor backhand.

The 1984 Olympics will be held in Los Angeles *even though* many of the city's residents do not want to have the games there.

Another very common error is the comma splice. Unlike a run-on, in which two independent clauses are run together with *no* punctuation, a **comma splice** consists of two independent clauses joined with *not enough* punctuation—that is, with only a comma (and *no* coordinate conjunction). The following are examples of comma splices.

I would like to visit Hawaii, I have many relatives there.
All my sisters have blue eyes, I do not.

A comma by itself is *not* a strong enough punctuation mark to separate two independent clauses. Only periods and semicolons can be used without conjunctions to separate independent clauses. Comma splices can be corrected by the same three methods used for correcting run-on sentences.

1. Divide the clauses into two separate sentences.

I would like to visit Hawaii. I have many relatives there.

All my sisters have blue eyes. I do not.

2. Make the sentence compound by adding either a coordinate conjunction *and* a comma or by adding a semicolon.

> I would like to visit Hawaii; I have many relatives there.
> All my sisters have blue eyes, *but* I do not.

3. Make the sentence complex by adding a subordinate conjunction.

> I would like to visit Hawaii *because* I have many relatives there.
> *Although* all my sisters have blue eyes, I do not.

Correct the following run-on sentences and comma splices.

Gary is used to cold weather, he grew up in Minnesota.

They are always in debt they have too many credit cards.

Comma splices are serious errors, you should avoid making them.

Sue has many problems she always manages to look cheerful.

EXERCISE 14A

Correct all the run-on sentences and comma splices in the following exercise. If a sentence is neither a run-on nor a comma splice, label it *C* for *correct*.

1. Most people are familiar with guide dogs for the blind, fewer know of "hearing-ear" dogs for the deaf.

2. Daily life can be difficult for the deaf common problems include the inability to hear an alarm clock or a knock at the door.

3. Dogs have been used for years to help the blind, now they are also being used to help the deaf.

4. Hearing-ear dogs are trained to respond to specific sounds they then lead their masters to the source of the noise.

5. For example, dogs may jump on their masters' beds at the sound of an alarm or pull them toward ringing telephones.

6. Hearing-ear dogs do not necessarily have pedigrees, nor are they limited to specific breeds.

7. However, good hearing-ear dogs must like working with people they must also be intelligent enough to undergo a rigorous training program.

8. The training program lasts for four months during this time they are taught how to work with the deaf.

9. Dogs must learn to distinguish between important and unimportant sounds.

10. For example, a fire alarm calls for an immediate response, the barking of another dog does not.

11. One of their most valuable services is to deaf parents of infant children, these people cannot hear their babies cry.

12. Hearing-ear dogs can alert parents to an infant's cries this relieves the parents from the need to keep a constant watch over their children.

13. Hearing-ear dogs have enabled many deaf people to lead less frustrating and more independent lives.

EXERCISE 14B

Correct all of the run-on sentences and comma splices in the following essay. Do *not* make changes in sentences which are already correctly punctuated.

Grunion are small silvery fish, they range in length from approximately five to eight inches. Each spring and summer they spawn on the beaches of Southern California. They arrive during the full moon, this is when the tide is highest. Incoming waves carry thousands of fish onto the beach. The eggs are laid and fertilized, then the grunion return to sea on the next wave.

This unusual method of breeding has led to the sport of grunion hunting. It is very different from other forms of fishing, no equipment can be used. In fact, state law requires that grunion be caught only with bare hands.

During the spring and summer, the dates of grunion runs are included in local weather forecasts. Most grunion runs occur at night. The most efficient way to catch grunion is to assemble a fairly large group of people this increases the chance of getting a good catch. The fishing party should arrive at the beach at least half an hour before the run is scheduled to begin in order to stake out a good location. It is best not to try to catch the very first fish that land on the beach, this may frighten other fish away. Once the main run has started, everyone should try to grab as many grunion as possible. Grunion are extremely slippery, a person can expect to lose almost as many grunion as he or she catches.

After the run is over, the grunion are cleaned and scaled and are ready to eat. They can be taken home, a better method is to grill or fry them on a portable barbeque right at the beach. Usually someone will have brought a salad and beverages to complete the meal.

There are many fish which taste better than the grunion, the appeal of a grunion hunt is in the challenge of catching the fish and in the fun of spending an evening at the beach with friends.

15 Avoiding Fragments

The basic unit of expression in written English is the sentence. As you already know, *a sentence must contain at least one independent clause.*

If you take a group of words which is *not* a complete sentence and punctuate it as though it were a complete sentence, you have created a **sentence fragment**. In other words, you have written only a piece—a fragment—of a sentence rather than a complete sentence.

As you can see. These three groups of words. Are fragments.

Although fragments occur frequently in speech and occasionally in informal writing, they are generally not acceptable in classroom writing and should be avoided in formal writing situations.

There are two types of fragments: **dependent clauses** and **phrases**.

As you have already learned in Lesson 13 (page 113), a dependent clause cannot stand alone as a complete sentence. It must be attached to an independent clause in order to form a complex sentence.

Therefore, any dependent clause which is not part of a complex sentence is a fragment.

Rewrite the following groups of words so that they no longer contain any fragments.

When we arrived at the theater. The movie had already begun.

We'll miss our plane. If we don't hurry.

I'm willing to help you. Whenever you have a problem.

(Are you remembering to punctuate your sentences correctly?)

The second type of fragment is the phrase. Since a **phrase** is defined as a group of words which does *not* contain both a subject and a verb, a phrase obviously cannot be a clause or a complete sentence. All phrases are fragments. Study the following fragments, and then notice the way each phrase has been changed from a fragment to a complete sentence.

FRAGMENT The car on the highway. (This phrase has a potential subject—car—but no verb.)

SENTENCE The car *stalled* on the highway.

FRAGMENT The ambulance speeding to the hospital. (This phrase lacks a complete verb. An -ing verb must be preceded by a helping verb. Or you may change the -ing verb form to a single main verb.)

SENTENCE The ambulance *was speeding* to the hospital.

or

The ambulance *sped* to the hospital.

FRAGMENT The neighbors irritated by our dog's barking. (As in the previous fragment, this phrase needs a helping verb in order to form a complete verb.)

SENTENCE The neighbors *are irritated* by our dog's barking.

When you are writing a composition, be careful not to separate a phrase from the rest of the sentence to which it belongs.

INCORRECT Be careful of dangerous rip tides. On the beach.

CORRECT Be careful of dangerous rip tides on the beach.

INCORRECT Amused by the joke. Jerry began to laugh.

CORRECT Amused by the joke, Jerry began to laugh.

INCORRECT We saw a long line of people. Waiting to get into the theater.

CORRECT We saw a long line of people waiting to get into the theater.

Rewrite the following items so that they no longer contain any fragments.

The weather being much too cold for swimming.

The baby tired and cranky from lack of sleep.

Pleased with the pianist's performance. The audience demanded an encore.

I burned my hand. While frying chicken for dinner.

To summarize: **phrases** are sentence fragments because they do not contain both a subject and a verb (in other words, they are not clauses). **Dependent clauses** are fragments because they are not *independent* clauses. This is simply another way of stating the most basic rule of sentence construction.

Every sentence must contain at least one independent clause.

EXERCISE 15A

Change each of the following fragments into a complete sentence.

1. A favorite dish in Spain being squid served in its own ink.

   _____

   _____

2. The flowers wilted by the heat.

   _____

   _____

3. When I get home tonight.

   _____

   _____

4. An unexpected spell of cold weather during August.

   _____

   _____

5. Because he sprained his ankle last week.

   _____

   _____

6. Riding the subway to work each morning.

   _____

   _____

7. The houses torn down to make room for a parking lot.

   _____

   _____

8. If you are left-handed.

   _____

   _____

9. The feel of sand under her feet and the ocean breeze blowing against her face. _____

   _____

   _____

10. Ever since I can remember.

    _____

    _____

11. Discouraged by his inability to find a job.

    _____

    _____

12. The elderly couple walking down the street arm in arm.

    _____

    _____

EXERCISE 15B

Correct any fragments which you find in the following exercise. If an item contains no fragments, label it *C* for *correct*.

1. When most Americans think of Indians. They picture the Indians of the Great Plains.

2. Countless painters having portrayed these Indians. As fearless warriors and great hunters.

3. Actually, the great age of the Plains Indians lasted for only two centuries.

4. Starting with the introduction of the horse at the beginning of the eighteenth century and ending with the defeat of the Indians by the United States Army at the end of the nineteenth century.

5. Before the Spanish brought horses to North America. Some Plains Indian tribes had already been nomadic buffalo hunters for thousands of years.

6. However, their mobility was limited. Because they used dogs as pack animals.

7. Dogs hauling burdens and people on foot carrying their household belongings could travel only five or six miles a day.

8. Moving camp was a difficult task. Especially for the aged, the women, and the children.

9. Horses gradually spread from Mexico and the Southwest to the Great Plains. Mainly through intertribal trading.

10. After a tribe acquired horses. Its way of life changed.

11. The most important changes being increased mobility, easier methods for hunting buffalo, and more opportunities for waging warfare against other tribes.

12. The Plains Indians perfected a lifestyle based on the horse. But were eventually defeated by a culture more technologically advanced than their own.

Compound and Complex Sentences Versus Run-On Sentences and Fragments   Unit Review

Correct any sentence fragments, run-on sentences, or comma splices which you find in the following essay.

If you want to feel like an explorer. You should visit Cabo da Roca, Portugal. Cabo da Roca is famous. Because it is the western-most point in continental Europe.

During the sixteenth century, Portugal was a major naval power, her ships sailed to Africa, Asia, and the Americas. To explore lands then unknown to most Europeans. The first ships to sail completely around the world being commanded by a Portuguese navigator. Named Ferdinand Magellan.

The Portuguese are proud of their history as explorers this is the reason that they have made Cabo da Roca a tourist site. Today you can drive to the small government tourist office at Cabo da Roca, from the office you walk several hundred feet to a steep cliff overlooking the sea. A strong wind nearly blows you off your feet such a wind once filled the sails of Portuguese ships bound for the New World. If you have a good imagination. You can almost picture ships anchored below.

When you return to the tourist office. You can purchase a souvenir of your visit to Cabo da Roca. It is a beautiful multi-colored certificate. Resembling an ancient handwritten manu-script. The official guide fills in your name and the date, then he signs the certificate and stamps it with sealing wax.

An English translation of the certificate (which you do not have to correct) reads:

This is to certify that (your name) has been to Cape Roca, Sintra, Portugal, the westernmost point in continental Europe, where the land ends and the sea begins. Here still reigns the spirit of faith and adventure which took the Portuguese caravels in search of new worlds for the world.

Punctuation

16 Parenthetical Expressions

When speaking, people often interrupt their sentences with expressions such as *by the way, after all,* or *as a matter of fact.* These expressions are not really part of the main idea of the sentence; instead, they are interrupting—or **parenthetical**—expressions which speakers use to fill in the pauses while they are thinking of what to say next. In speech, people indicate that these parenthetical expressions are not part of the main idea of the sentence by pausing and dropping their voices before and after the expression. In writing, the same pauses are indicated with commas.

You have already learned that commas may be used to separate the clauses in compound and complex sentences. Another major function of the comma is to set off interrupting or **parenthetical expressions** from the rest of the sentence in which they occur.

Read the following sentences aloud, and notice how the commas around the italicized parenthetical expressions correspond to the pauses you make in speech.

Well, it's time for us to leave.
Carolyn is, *on the whole*, a very good tennis player.
The rent is due tomorrow, *isn't it*?

The rule for punctuating parenthetical expressions is very simple:

A parenthetical expression must be completely set off from the rest of the sentence by commas.

This means that if the parenthetical expression occurs at the *beginning* of the sentence, it is *followed* by a comma. For example:

Yes, I understand your problem.

If the parenthetical expression is at the *end* of the sentence, it is *preceded* by a comma.

The airline will locate your luggage soon, *I hope.*

If the parenthetical expression is in the *middle* of the sentence, it is both *preceded* and *followed* by a comma.

Diamonds and graphite, *for example*, are both forms of carbon.

There are many parenthetical expressions. Some of the most frequently used ones are listed below.

after all

as a matter of fact

at any rate

etc. (an abbreviation of the Latin words *et cetera*, meaning "and other things")

for example

for instance

however

in fact

nevertheless

of course

on the other hand

on the whole

therefore

well (at the beginning of a sentence)

yes and *no* (at the beginning of a sentence)

Expressions such as the following are often parenthetical if they occur in a position *other than* at the beginning of a sentence:

> doesn't it
>
> isn't it
>
> I believe
>
> I suppose
>
> I think
>
> that is
>
> you know

For example:

It always rains the day after I wash my car, *doesn't it?*
Today, *you know*, is the last day to drop a class without receiving a failing grade.

Continual repetition of the parenthetical expression *you know* should be avoided in both speech and writing. If you are speaking clearly and your listener is paying attention, he knows what you are saying and does not have to be constantly reminded of the fact. Besides, you know, continually repeating *you know* can be irritating to your listener; and, you know, it doesn't really accomplish anything.

Study the following points carefully.

1. Some of the above words and phrases can be either parenthetical or not parenthetical, depending upon how they are used in a sentence. **If an expression is parenthetical, it can be removed from the sentence, and the remaining words will still be a complete sentence.**

PARENTHETICAL She is, *after all*, only a child.
NOT PARENTHETICAL The doctors couldn't save the patient's life even *after all* their efforts.
PARENTHETICAL I've met you before, *I believe.*
NOT PARENTHETICAL *I believe* that you are telling me the truth.

2. Since the abbreviation *etc.* is parenthetical, it must be *preceded and followed* by a comma if it occurs in the middle of a sentence.

Greeting cards, stationery, gift wrap, *etc.*, are sold at Hallmark shops.

The final comma after *etc.* indicates that *etc.* is parenthetical. Notice that this comma serves a different function from the commas which separate the items in the series.

3. Some parenthetical expressions, like *however* and *nevertheless,* frequently join the clauses in a compound sentence. They should be punctuated as follows:

> I cared for the plant carefully; *however*, it withered and died.
> The university is located in the middle of a desert; *nevertheless,* each of its students must pass a swimming test in order to graduate.

The semicolon is needed because the clauses in the compound sentence are not joined by a coordinate conjunction (see page 103). The semicolon also takes the place of the comma which would normally precede a parenthetical expression occurring in the middle of a sentence. A comma follows the parenthetical expression to set it off from the remainder of the sentence.

4. People's names and titles are also set off by commas **if you are speaking directly to them** in a sentence. This type of construction is called **direct address**. The punctuation of direct address is the same as that used for parenthetical expressions.

> Hail, *Caesar*!
> Please, *children*, wipe your feet before you enter the house.
> *Ladies and gentlemen*, the meeting will now begin.

Notice that names and titles are set off by commas only when the person is being *directly addressed* in the sentence. Otherwise, no commas are needed.

> My neighbor's name is Gail. (no comma)
> *Gail*, has the mail come yet? (direct address)
> Dr. Howard is an expert on Shakespeare. (no comma)
> *Dr. Howard*, may I see you during your office hours? (direct address)

EXERCISE 16A

Part One Add commas to the following sentences wherever they are necessary. If a sentence needs no additional punctuation, label it *C* for *correct*. The sentences in this section of the exercise deal only with the punctuation of parenthetical expressions.

1. A comma is used to set off a parenthetical expression at the beginning or end of a sentence isn't it?

2. However a parenthetical expression in the middle of a sentence must be both preceded and followed by a comma.

3. The rule of course is that a parenthetical expression must be completely set off from the rest of the sentence by commas.

4. This is on the whole an easy punctuation rule to follow.

5. After all the commas used with parenthetical expressions usually correspond to the pauses that occur in ordinary speech.

Part Two Add commas and semicolons to the following sentences wherever they are necessary. If a sentence needs no additional punctuation, label it *C* for *correct*. This section covers the punctuation of compound and complex sentences as well as parenthetical expressions.

6. Of all the fish that inhabit the Amazon River in South America, the most dangerous on the whole is the piranha.

7. I believe that the name "piranha" comes from two Indian words meaning "fish" and "tooth."

8. As a matter of fact the piranha has twenty-eight razor-sharp teeth.

9. There are more than twenty species of piranha however only four are considered to be dangerous to man.

10. Although most piranhas are less than a foot long the fact that they swim in large swarms does of course increase the danger they pose.

11. For example even a thick-skinned alligator can easily be eaten by a school of hungry piranhas.

12. Unusual fish appeal to collectors therefore piranhas used to be sold in tropical fish stores throughout the United States.

13. Now however many states restrict the importation and sale of piranhas.

14. Piranhas are not native to the United States nevertheless the danger exists that they may escape and infest local waterways.

15. The idea of having piranhas in our lakes and streams is frightening isn't it?

EXERCISE 16B

Add commas and semicolons to the following sentences wherever they are necessary. If a sentence needs no additional punctuation, label it *C* for *correct*. This exercise covers the punctuation of compound and complex sentences and parenthetical expressions.

1. One of the relics from the age of travel by horse and buggy is the covered bridge.

2. Covered bridges are usually associated with New England however they are equally as common in northeastern Canada.

3. Covered bridges are usually completely covered that is they have both side walls and a roof.

4. In fact covered bridges resemble long tunnels covered with barns.

5. Many people believe that covered bridges were designed to keep snow off the bridge floor this theory however is incorrect.

6. As a matter of fact snow was deliberately spread on the floors of covered bridges during the winter to make travel by sleigh and bob-sled possible.

7. Bridges were actually covered for protection against the sun and rain since exposure to these elements would of course eventually rot the bridge's timbers.

8. A covered bridge had an average life expectancy of eighty years on the other hand an uncovered bridge usually lasted only ten years.

9. Because a common method of courting (dating) in the 19th century was for couples to take buggy rides together covered bridges also helped to promote romance by providing a stopping place for the buggy.

10. In New Brunswick for example covered bridges were often referred to as "kissing bridges."

11. In fact some horses became so used to being driven on romantic rides that they automatically stopped (without command) once they set foot inside the bridge.

12. This habit could of course prove embarrassing when the horse was used on other occasions for instance taking the family to church.

13. I believe one of the best places to see covered bridges is the province of New Brunswick in northeastern Canada.

14. The Tourist Office in New Brunswick will provide you with a list of all the province's covered bridges and their locations therefore you can plan your trip to see as many bridges as possible.

17 Appositives

In sentences you sometimes use a noun whose meaning may not be as clear to your reader as it is to you. For example, suppose that you write:

Fiat automobiles are manufactured in Turin.

If you think that your reader does not know where Turin is, you may add a phrase to your sentence to provide further information about Turin.

Fiat automobiles are manufactured in Turin, *a city in northeastern Italy*.

This kind of explanatory phrase is called an **appositive** (from the verb *to appose*, meaning "to place things beside each other"). An appositive is a phrase placed beside a noun in order to clarify that noun's meaning. Study the following sentences, in which the appositives have been italicized. Notice that each appositive immediately follows the noun it describes.

The komondor, *a Hungarian sheepdog*, has a coat that looks like a mop.
Balboa, *a 16th-century Spanish explorer*, was the first European to discover the American side of the Pacific Ocean.

In Europe, fruits and vegetables are usually sold by the kilogram, *an amount equal to 2.2 pounds.*

As you can see, appositives must be set off by commas from the rest of the sentence just as parenthetical expressions are. Appositives are considered *extra* elements in a sentence because they add additional information about a noun which has already been specifically identified. For example, in the first sentence above, even without the appositive "a Hungarian sheepdog," you know which dog has fur that looks like a mop because the dog has been specifically identified as a *komondor.* In the second sentence, even without the appositive "a 16th-century Spanish explorer," you know that the person who discovered the Pacific Ocean was *Balboa.* And in the third sentence, even without the appositive "an amount equal to 2.2 pounds," you know that the unit of weight used to sell produce in Europe is the *kilogram.*

Here is the rule for punctuating this kind of explanatory phrase or clause:

If a phrase or clause adds additional information about a noun that has already been specifically identified, that phrase or clause must be completely set off from the rest of the sentence by commas.

(In this lesson, you will be dealing with appositives, which are phrases. In Lesson 18, you will be applying the same rule to clauses.)

Specifically identified includes mentioning either a person's first or last name, or both, or using words such as "my oldest brother," "my ten o'clock class on Monday," or "my hometown." The nouns in these last three phrases are considered to be *specifically identified* because even though you have not mentioned your brother's name, you can have only one "oldest" brother. Similarly, only one specific class can be your "ten o'clock class on Monday," and only one specific town can be your "hometown." In other words, *specifically identified* means limiting the meaning of a general word like "town" to *one particular* town or limiting a general word like "class" to *one particular* class.

Underline the appositives in the following sentences, and then punctuate them. Remember that appositives *follow* the nouns which they describe.

My oldest brother an orthopedic surgeon spends much of his time

treating the injuries of high school athletes. (In this sentence you should have placed commas before and after "an orthopedic surgeon.")

My ten o'clock class on Monday Chemistry I is my most difficult course.

Last summer I visited my hometown Detroit, Michigan.

On the other hand, if a phrase is *necessary* to establish the specific identity of a noun, it is *not* set off by commas. Study the difference between the following sentences:

The novel *Great Expectations* is considered by many critics to be Charles Dickens' greatest work. (No commas are used to set off *Great Expectations* because the title is necessary to identify which of Dickens' novels is considered to be his greatest work.)
Dickens' fourteenth novel, *Great Expectations*, is considered by many critics to be his greatest work. (Commas are used to set off *Great Expectations* because Dickens' greatest work has already been identified as his *fourteenth novel.*)

Most single-word appositives are necessary to establish the specific identity of the nouns they follow and are, therefore, *not* set off by commas.

My cousin *Rose* lives in New York City.
The word *penurious* means "stingy."

EXERCISE 17A

Add commas to the following sentences wherever they are necessary.

1. The appositives in this exercise describe places in Hawaii our fiftieth state.

2. Honolulu the capital of Hawaii means "protected bay" in Hawaiian.

3. Pearl Harbor the Hawaiian Island's major naval base was named for the pearl oysters formerly found there.

4. Punchbowl the National Cemetery of the Pacific is located in the crater of a dormant volcano.

5. Tourists can ski on Hawaii's highest mountain Mauna Kea (13,796 feet).

6. "White mountain" the English translation of Mauna Kea refers to the fact that the mountain is often snowcapped.

7. Waikiki the most famous of Hawaii's resort areas was once worthless swampland.

8. Another famous beach is Makaha the site of many international surfing contests.

9. The Iolani Palace the only royal palace in the United States is used as a setting for the television series "Hawaii Five-0." (In real life, there are no police offices in the Iolani Palace.)

10. The Polynesian Cultural Center one of Hawaii's major tourist attractions was established by the Church of Jesus Christ of Latter Day Saints (the Mormons) to provide jobs for students attending the Church College of Hawaii and to preserve the culture of the Polynesian Islands.

11. The Bishop Museum Hawaii's world-famous museum of natural history was built in memory of Bernice Pauahi Bishop a 19th-century Hawaiian princess. (Notice that this sentence has two appositives.)

12. The Parker Ranch one of the world's largest cattle ranches covers 185,610 acres on the island of Hawaii.

EXERCISE 17B

Add commas and semicolons to the following sentences wherever they are necessary. If a sentence needs no additional punctuation, label it *C* for *correct*. This exercise covers punctuation rules from previous lessons as well as the punctuation of appositives.

1. Each weekday morning I set out on my own mini-tour of Los Angeles.

2. My trip begins in West Los Angeles an area of the city near the Pacific Ocean.

3. I turn left onto Olympic Boulevard one of the city's main east-west arteries.

4. As I travel east on Olympic I cross Westwood Boulevard a street leading directly into the campus of UCLA.

5. Further east, I pass Century City a carefully planned, very modern collection of shopping malls, office buildings, and high-rise apartments.

6. Beverly Hills one of the wealthiest cities in Southern California is carefully set off from the city of Los Angeles.

7. Although I am still on Olympic Boulevard the street signs in Beverly Hills are a different color than those in Los Angeles and the surface of the road is noticeably smoother.

8. Trees line both sides of Beverly Hills' portion of Olympic Boulevard in fact the landscaping laws are so strict that every car dealer's lot is hidden from view by rows of shrubs.

9. Soon the road feels bumpy again therefore I know that I have left Beverly Hills and am back in Los Angeles.

10. I pass a series of synagogues and Hebrew schools as I near Fairfax Avenue the center of Los Angeles' Jewish community.

11. After another two miles, I turn north on the corner of Olympic and Rimpau the site of the oldest high school in Los Angeles.

12. As I continue driving north I pass through Hancock Park an elegant neighborhood with stately homes that look like small mansions.

13. I turn east onto Melrose Avenue and pass by Paramount Studios and several radio stations however I am not yet in Hollywood.

14. If I were to continue driving either north or east I would be in Hollywood the former "home of the stars."

15. But because I have a job to do I turn left on the corner of Melrose and Heliotrope the western boundary of Los Angeles City College and begin another day of teaching.

18 Restrictive and Nonrestrictive Clauses

In Lesson 17 you learned that if a phrase adds extra information about a noun which has already been specifically identified, that phrase (an **appositive**) must be set off by commas. For example:

Many of NBC's television shows arc filmed in Burbank, *a city in the San Fernando Valley.*

The appositive is set off by commas because the place in which many of NBC's television shows are filmed has already been specifically identified as *Burbank.*

On the other hand, if a phrase is *necessary* to establish the specific identity of a noun, the phrase is *not* set off by commas.

The verb *to be* is the most irregular verb in the English language.

The phrase *to be* is not set off by commas because it is necessary to identify which specific verb is the most irregular verb in the English language.

The same rule that applies to the punctuation of appositive phrases also applies to the punctuation of *clauses.* Read the following sentences, in which the dependent clauses have been italicized. Can you see why one sentence in each pair has commas while the other does not?

The woman *whom you have just met* is in charge of the project.
Teresa Gomez, *whom you have just met*, is in charge of the project.
The book *which I am now reading* is an anthology of Afro-American literature.
Black Voices, which I am now reading, is an anthology of Afro-American literature.

In the first sentence of each pair, the dependent clause is necessary to establish the specific identity of the noun it follows. This type of clause is called a **restrictive clause** because it *restricts*, or limits, the meaning of the word it describes. For example, in the first sentence if the restrictive clause were removed, the sentence would read.

The woman is in charge of the project.

The meaning of this sentence is unclear since there are millions of women in the world, and any one of them might be in charge of the project. But when the clause is added to the sentence, the meaning of the general word "woman" is now *restricted*, or limited, to *one particular* woman—*the woman whom you have just met*. Thus, the restrictive clause "whom you have just met" establishes the specific identity of the word "woman."

Similarly, in the third sentence, the clause "which I am now reading" identifies *which* book is an anthology of Afro-American literature. It restricts the general word "book" to *one particular* book—*the book which I am now reading*.

Since restrictive clauses are necessary to establish the specific identity of the nouns they describe, the following punctuation rule applies:

Restrictive clauses are *not* set off by commas.

In contrast, the clauses in the second and fourth sentences are *not* necessary to identify which particular woman is in charge of the project or which particular book is an anthology of Afro-American literature. In these sentences, the woman has already been identified as Teresa Gomez, and the book has already been identified as *Black Voices*. Since these clauses are *not* restrictive clauses, they are called **nonrestrictive clauses**. Nonrestrictive clauses merely add extra information about the nouns they describe. They serve the same function as appositives (see page 146) and are punctuated in the same way.

Nonrestrictive clauses must be completely set off from the rest of the sentence by commas.

This means that if a nonrestrictive clause is at the *end* of a sentence, it will be *preceded* by a comma. If it is in the *middle* of a sentence, it will be both *preceded and followed* by a comma. (Like appositives, nonrestrictive clauses never occur at the beginning of a sentence since they must follow the noun which they describe.)

The restrictive and nonrestrictive clauses which you have been studying are called **adjective clauses** because, like adjectives, these clauses describe nouns. The words which most frequently introduce adjective clauses are:

that

which

who

whom

whose

Like all clauses, adjective clauses must contain both a subject and a verb. But notice that in adjective clauses *the word which introduces the clause may also be the subject of the clause.*

                      s   v

The house *which once occupied this lot* was destroyed by fire.

Or the clause may contain a separate subject:

                    s v

The wallet *that I lost* contained all my credit cards.

Adjective clauses, like adverb clauses (see page 112), are used in **complex sentences**. Although these sentences may not seem to be complex at first glance, if you study the sentences below, you will see that each of them has two subjects and two verbs. Also, if the adjective clause, which is the **dependent clause**, is removed, a complete independent clause remains.

> I don't care for the music *that you are playing.*
> New Brunswick, *which is one of Canada's Maritime Provinces,* is known as the "Picture Province" because of its beautiful scenery. (Adjective clauses often occur in the middle of a sentence since they must follow the noun they describe. In this sentence, part of the independent clause precedes the adjective clause, and the remainder follows it. The independent clause is "New Brunswick is known as the 'Picture Province' because of its beautiful scenery.")

Andre Watts, *who is one of my favorite pianists*, is giving a recital tonight.

Underline the adjective clause in each of the following sentences, and circle the noun which it describes. Then decide which clauses are restrictive (and need no commas) and which clauses are nonrestrictive (and do need commas). Add the appropriate punctuation. (Note: The word *that* introduces only *restrictive* clauses.)

Union Square which is one of San Francisco's main shopping areas is known for its open-air flower stalls.

The classes that I am taking this semester are all easy for me.

Most tourists who come to Los Angeles also visit Disneyland which is less than an hour's drive from the city. (Notice that a sentence may contain more than one adjective clause.)

The candidate whom we supported was not elected.

Ms. Lindquist whose native language is Swedish also speaks French, German, and English.

EXERCISE 18A

Part One Construct complex sentences of your own using the words listed below to form *restrictive* clauses. Underline the adjective clause in each of your sentences, and circle the noun it describes.

1. who: _____

_____

2. which: _____

_____

3. whose: _____

_____

4. that: _____

_____

Part Two Construct complex sentences of your own using the words listed below to form *nonrestrictive* clauses. Underline the adjective clause in each of your sentences, and circle the noun it describes. Use appropriate punctuation.

5. who: _____

_____

6. which: _____

_____

7. whose:_____

_____

8. whom:_____

_____

Part Three Underline the adjective clauses in the following sentences, and circle the word which each clause describes. If the clause is nonrestrictive, add the necessary punctuation. If the clause is restrictive, the sentence needs no additional punctuation, so label it *C* for *correct*.

9. Everyone who visits London should try to see the British Museum.

10. The British Museum contains treasures that were collected by British archaeologists from all parts of the world.

11. One very famous collection of sculptures is the Elgin Marbles which were brought to England from the Parthenon at the beginning of the 19th century.

12. Perhaps the most famous single artifact in the museum is the Rosetta Stone whose inscriptions in Egyptian and Greek enabled scholars to learn to read Egyptian hieroglyphics.

13. The Mildenhall Treasure which was discovered in 1942 is a collection of Roman silver dating back to the Roman occupation of Britain during the first through the fifth centuries A.D.

14. The British Museum is also a world-famous library that contains a copy of every book published in Britain since 1757, along with many other older rare books and manuscripts.

EXERCISE 18B

Add commas and semicolons to the following sentences wherever they are needed. If a sentence needs no additional punctuation, label it *C* for *correct*. Sentences 1–6 deal only with the punctuation of adjective clauses. Notice that some sentences may contain more than one adjective clause. The remainder of the exercise includes constructions which you have studied in previous lessons.

1. One of London's most famous tourist attractions is the Tower of London which was originally built in the 11th century by William the Conqueror.

2. One thing that makes the Tower interesting is the many famous people who were imprisoned in it.

3. They include Anne Boleyn and Catherine Howard who were the second and fifth of Henry VIII's six wives.

4. Anne and Catherine who were both charged with adultery were two of the many people who were beheaded in the yard outside the Tower.

5. Today a plaque lists the names of some of the victims whose lives were ended here by the executioner's axe.

6. A murder which still horrifies people after nearly 500 years was the killing in 1483 of the two young sons and heirs (aged twelve and nine) of King Edward IV.

7. Although some doubt exists about the circumstances of the children's death the person who would have profited the most by their deaths was King Richard III the children's uncle.

8. In 1674 the skeletons of two children were discovered during alterations in the Tower they are generally believed to be the secretly buried remains of King Edward's sons.

9. However not all of the Tower is associated with deaths and imprisonments.

10. The Tower is also the home of the Crown Jewels which are among Britain's greatest treasures.

11. Stored here are crowns and scepters that the Queen uses only on state occasions for example the opening of Parliament.

12. One of the most famous jewels is the Kohinoor Diamond which is one of the largest diamonds in the world.

19 Items in a Series and Dates and Addresses

A **series** consists of *three or more* items. Commas are placed between each item in a series in order to separate the items from each other. The final comma before the conjunction is optional.

Danish, Swedish, and *Norwegian* are related languages.

or

Danish, Swedish and *Norwegian* are related languages.

If *every* item in a series is joined by a conjunction (*and, or,* or *nor*), no commas are needed since the conjunctions keep the individual items separated. This type of construction is used only when the writer wishes to place particular emphasis on the number of items in the series.

Soup and *salad* and *dessert* are included in the price of your meal.

If a date or address consists of more than one item, a comma is used after each part of the date or address, *including a comma after the last item.* Notice that this punctuation rule differs from that used for an ordinary series.

My grandparents will celebrate their fiftieth wedding anniversary on October 11, 1980, with a party for all of their family.

We moved from Norman, Oklahoma, to Flagstaff, Arizona, in 1975.

If a date or address consists of only a single item, no comma is necessary.

October 31st is Hallowe'en. (The name and day of a month are considered a single item.)
Neiman Marcus has stores in Dallas and Beverly Hills.

A comma is not used before a zip code number.

The official mailing address for Hollywood is Los Angeles, California 90028.

Punctuate the following sentences:

The armistice signed on November 11 1918 ended the fighting in World War One.

Because of the multi-ethnic character of my neighborhood, church bazaars sell tacos pizza teriyaki chow mein and hot dogs.

The coffee shop's special club sandwich contains ham and cheese and turkey.

I can't believe that you drove from Portland Oregon to Newark New Jersey in three days.

EXERCISE 19A

Add commas to the following sentences wherever they are needed. If a sentence needs no additional punctuation, label it *C* for *correct*.

1. A "Continental breakfast" consists of juice coffee and a roll.

2. Tours of Italy nearly always include the cities of Rome Venice and Florence.

3. September weather in Los Angeles is often hot dry and smoggy. (Notice that adjectives, as well as nouns, can be used in a series.)

4. The cheerleaders jumped and screamed and laughed with joy when their team won the game. (Verbs, as well as other parts of speech, such as adverbs, can also form a series.)

5. The park ranger approached the skunks slowly quietly and cautiously.

6. William of Normandy defeated King Harold II of England on October 14 1066 at the Battle of Hastings.

7. Tuesday October 29 1929 was the day that the stock market crashed.

8. He worked in Kansas City Missouri and Chicago Illinois before his company transferred him to New York City.

9. I lived in Detroit and Honolulu before I moved to Portland.

10. She plans to buy a Volkswagen Rabbit a Honda Civic or a Dodge Omni.

EXERCISE 19B

Add commas and semicolons to the following sentences wherever they are needed. If a sentence needs no additional punctuation, label it *C* for *correct*. This exercise includes material from previous lessons.

1. As the deadline for her manuscript approached the author became tired discouraged and exasperated.

2. A New England boiled dinner usually includes corned beef cabbage potatoes and beets.

3. I would like to own a cocker spaniel my children want a Great Dane or a St. Bernard or a German shepherd.

4. The Los Angeles County Fair is held in Pomona California during the month of September.

5. Queen Victoria died on January 22 1901 after the longest reign (sixty-four years) of any British monarch.

6. The address of the San Carlos Hotel is 150 East 50th Street New York New York 10022.

7. It is small comfortable and conveniently located however its prices are rather expensive.

8. I plan to attend an English conference in Washington D.C. this March.

9. Authentic chili con carne contains beef chili peppers and a little cornmeal it does not contain any beans.

10. We drove across Canada from Victoria British Columbia to Montreal Quebec during our summer vacation.

Punctuation
Unit Review

Add commas and semicolons (no periods) to the following sentences wherever they are necessary.

A plant that is considered valuable in one country can be a pest in another. A good example of this phenomenon is the vine which is known as *kuzu* in Japan and "kudzu" in the United States.

In Japan which is its native country kudzu is a highly prized wild plant that grows mainly in mountainous regions. Its leaves vines shoots flowers and roots are all put to use none of the plant is wasted.

In the United States on the other hand kudzu is often regarded as a nuisance. Kudzu was first brought to the United States in 1876 and it now grows throughout the Deep South. In fact the main objection which many Southerners have to kudzu is its amazing ability to grow. The South's climate is much more favorable for kudzu than Japan's and most Japanese would be astonished by the growth rate of American kudzu. For example under ideal conditions kudzu can grow one foot a day or up to one hundred feet in a single season. When kudzu runs out of room to grow on the ground it starts to grow skyward. Kudzu destroys valuable timber by climbing up trees and smothering them with its dense foliage. It climbs power poles and shorts out transmission lines. It covers road signs and pulls down telephone poles. Worst of all however is its sneaky habit of invading farmland and destroying crops. James Dickey a noted Southern writer has gone so far as to call kudzu "a vegetable form of cancer."

Since kudzu is a wild plant it grows without fertilizer irrigation or any care at all. In fact one of the South's most difficult problems is to find a way to kill kudzu. Only the most toxic of herbicides can destroy kudzu however these herbicides leave the land unfit for growing other crops for many months. Many Southerners resort to seemingly endless attempts to chop down dig up plow under and burn kudzu.

Is there a solution to the kudzu problem? Well in Japan powdered kudzu roots are used in traditional herbal medicines and in many kinds of food for example kudzu noodles kudzu tea kudzu gelatin and kudzu candy. Kudzu leaves shoots and flowers are eaten as vegetables. Kudzu vines are used to make rope and to weave textiles. Kudzu is also used for hay and silage.

Perhaps the United States could also learn to process kudzu into useful products then it would be able to make a profit from a plant which is now considered to be a pest.

An excellent book which describes the many uses of kudzu is *The Book of Kudzu* by William Shurtleff and Akiko Aoyagi. It is published by Autumn Press 7 Littell Road Brookline Massachusetts 02146.

Capitalization, Placement of Modifiers, and Parallel Structure

20 Capitalization

The general principle behind capitalization is that **proper nouns** (names of *specific* persons, places, or things) are capitalized. **Common nouns** (names of *general* persons, places, or things) are *not* capitalized.

Study the following sentences, each of which illustrates a rule of capitalization.

1. Capitalize all parts of a person's name.

   His favorite author is *E*dgar *A*llan *P*oe.

2. Capitalize the titles of relatives only when the titles precede the the person's name or when they take the place of a person's name.

   Today is *A*unt *G*race's birthday.
   There is a telephone call for you, *M*other.
   but
   My *a*unt and my *m*other are both retired.

   The same rule applies to professional titles.

   I have an appointment with *D*r. Gunter this afternoon.
   You should have a *d*octor examine your eyes.

3. Capitalize the names of streets, cities, and states.

> My nephew lives at 48 *B*oulder *A*venue,
> *W*innemucca, *N*evada.

4. Capitalize the names of countries, languages, and ethnic groups.

> Both *F*rench and *F*lemish are spoken in *B*elgium; the French speakers are called *W*alloons.

5. Capitalize the names of specific buildings, geographical features, schools, and other institutions.

> During our cruise on the *E*ast *R*iver, we could see the *S*tatue of *L*iberty, the *B*rooklyn *B*ridge, the *U*nited *N*ations, and *R*oosevelt *I*sland.

6. Capitalize the days of the week, the months of the year, and the names of holidays. Do *not* capitalize the names of the seasons of the year.

> *L*abor *D*ay is on *M*onday, *S*eptember 3rd.
> I plan to go to Europe in the *s*ummer.

7. Capitalize directions of the compass only when they refer to specific regions.

> Many American Indian tribes have reservations in the *S*outhwest.
>
> but
>
> The restaurant is on the *s*outhwest corner of Olympic and Barrington.

8. Capitalize the names of companies and brand names but not the names of the products themselves.

> *G*eneral *M*ills manufactures *B*etty *C*rocker *c*ake *m*ixes.

9. Capitalize the first word of every sentence.

10. Capitalize the subject pronoun "I."

11. Capitalize the first word of a title and all other words in the title except for articles (*a, an, the*) and except for conjunctions and prepositions which have fewer than five letters.

> The novel *All Quiet on the Western Front* deals with the experiences of a German soldier during World War I.

12. Capitalize the names of academic subjects only if they are already proper nouns or if they are common nouns followed by a course number.

> Her schedule of classes includes *c*alculus, *E*nglish, and *P*sychology 21.

13. Capitalize the names of specific historical events, such as wars, revolutions, religious and political movements, and specific eras.

> The *R*oaring *T*wenties came to an end with the start of the *D*epression.
> Martin Luther was a key figure in the *P*rotestant *R*eformation.

EXERCISE 20A

Add capital letters to the following sentences wherever they are necessary.

1. the basques live in the pyrenees mountains.

2. this region includes portions of both southern france and northern spain.

3. the basque language, which is known as eskuara, seems unrelated to any other european language.

4. many basques have immigrated to the united states to work as sheepherders.

5. most of them live in the west, especially in california and nevada.

6. an excellent basque restaurant is in the noriega hotel, 525 summer street, bakersfield, california.

7. one of my favorite novels is margaret craven's *i heard the owl call my name*, which deals with the life of canadian indians in the pacific northwest.

8. my birthday is on wednesday, october 31st, which is also hallowe'en.

9. rice krispies cereal is produced by the kellogg company, which is located in battle creek, michigan.

10. didn't uncle clarence say that professor campbell of stanford university was an old friend of his?

11. after he finishes chemistry 1B, fred will take a course in physics.

12. gettysburg, pennsylvania, is the site of one of the most important battles of the civil war.

EXERCISE 20B

Add capital letters to the following sentences wherever they are necessary.

1. he bought an underwood typewriter from a store called office supplies unlimited.

2. i took my mother and my grandmother out to dinner on mother's day.

3. most tourists in rome try to see the coliseum, the forum, and the trevi fountain.

4. on sunday we drove to solvang, a danish village and tourist attraction 150 miles north of los angeles.

5. charles dickens' novel *a tale of two cities* is set during the french revolution.

6. if your own doctor is not in, you may see doctor miller instead.

7. revere rubber bands are made by plymouth rubber company of canton, massachusetts.

8. before you enroll in zoology 12, you should take an introductory course in biology.

9. among the most common navajo surnames are begay and yazzie.

10. many people vacation in the northeast during the fall, when the leaves change colors.

21 Misplaced and Dangling Modifiers

Modifiers are words that are used to describe other words in a sentence. A modifier may be a single word, a phrase, or a clause. (Adjective clauses are discussed in Lesson 18.) Examples of some of the more common types of modifiers are given below. Circle the word which each italicized modifier describes.

adjective: He drank a cup of *black* coffee.

prepositional phrase: The woman *in the long blue dress* is the bride's

mother.

Another type of modifier is a participial phrase. A **participle** is a verb form which functions as an adjective. There are two kinds of participles. **Present participles** are formed by adding *-ing* to the main verb (for example, *walking, knowing, having*). **Past participles** are the verb forms which are used with the helping verb *have* (have *walked*, have *known*, have *had*). Circle the word which each participial phrase modifies.

participial phrases: *Wanting to earn some extra money*, Maria decided

to get a part-time job.

Mrs. Howard, *worried about the high crime rate in her neighborhood*, decided to buy a guard dog.

When you have circled the words which these modifiers describe, you will notice that although modifiers sometimes precede and sometimes follow the words they describe, they are in all cases placed as close to the word which they describe as possible. Failure to place a modifier in the appropriate position in a sentence results in an error known as a **misplaced modifier**.

MISPLACED He told a joke to his friends *that no one liked.*

CORRECT He told a joke *that no one liked* to his friends.

MISPLACED Sue always uses pencils for her math exams *with extremely fine points.*

CORRECT Sue always uses pencils *with extremely fine points* for her math exams.

Correct the misplaced modifiers in the following sentences.

Elaine bought a dress at a store that was on sale for twenty-five dollars.

The winner is the candidate in the election with the most votes.

A related kind of error is the **dangling modifier**. Dangling modifiers usually occur when a modifier is at the beginning of a sentence. Such modifiers describe the subject of the following clause. If the subject of the clause cannot logically perform the action described by the modifier, the modifier is said to "dangle."

DANGLING *While washing her hair*, a salesman knocked at Gail's door. (This sentence suggests that the salesman was washing Gail's hair while at the same time knocking at her door.)

CORRECT While *Gail* was washing her hair, a salesman knocked at her door.

DANGLING *Hoping to improve his game*, his tennis racket was restrung. (This sentence suggests that the tennis racket was trying to improve his game.)

CORRECT Hoping to improve his game, *he* had his tennis racket restrung.

Notice that there are several ways to correct dangling modifiers. You may add a noun or pronoun to the sentence to provide a word which the modifier can logically describe, or you may reword the entire sentence. *However, simply reversing the order of the dangling modifier and the rest of the sentence does not correct the error.*

DANGLING While trying to cook dinner, my steak was burned.
STILL DANGLING My steak was burned while trying to cook dinner.
CORRECT While I was trying to cook dinner, I burned the steak.

Because misplaced and dangling modifiers tend to create confusing and even absurd sentences, you should be careful to avoid them in your writing.

EXERCISE 21A

Part One Construct five sentences of your own, using the modifiers listed below at the beginning of your sentences. Make certain that your modifiers do not dangle.

1. Not having enough money with me, _____

_____

2. After jogging for three miles, _____

_____

3. By using public transportation instead of driving a car, _____

_____

4. In order to make friends, _____

_____

5. While waiting for the red light to change, _____

_____

Part Two Rewrite each of the following sentences so that none contains a misplaced or dangling modifier.

6. A Girl Scout came to my house to sell me cookies with an eager smile.

_____

_____

7. She exchanged her dollars in a French bank for francs.

_____

_____

8. After being sprayed by a skunk, the boy should bathe his dog in tomato juice.

_____

_____

9. Not being familiar with the freeway system, the car exited at the wrong off-ramp.

_____

_____

10. While waiting for the bus, it began to rain.

_____

_____

11. My budget was ruined after buying a new winter coat.

_____

_____

EXERCISE 21B

Some of the following sentences contain misplaced or dangling modifiers. Rewrite these sentences. If a sentence does not contain a misplaced or a dangling modifier, label it *C* for *correct*.

1. The television commercial showed a young woman driving a sports car with long blonde hair.

   _____

   _____

2. To learn grammar, the rules must be studied.

   _____

   _____

3. Wanting to be picked up and carried, the baby began to cry.

   _____

   _____

4. After applying a solution of baking soda and water to the car's battery terminals, the acid deposits disappeared.

   _____

   _____

5. To preserve its juiciness, salt should be added to a roast after it has been cooked.

_____

_____

6. Seeing spots before her eyes, waves of dizziness swept over her.

_____

_____

7. While playing the finale of the *1812 Overture*, cannons boomed and firecrackers exploded.

_____

_____

8. The hostess served crab legs to her guests that were dipped in melted butter.

_____

_____

9. After handling fish, a slice of lemon will remove the odor from your hands.

_____

_____

22 Parallel Structure

The term **parallel structure** means that similar ideas should be expressed in similar grammatical structures. For example:

The fortune teller said that my future husband would be *tall, dark,* and *handsome.*

The preceding sentence illustrates parallel structure. It contains three words which describe my future husband, and all three of these words have the same grammatical structure (they are all adjectives). In contrast, the following sentence does *not* have parallel structure.

The fortune teller said that my future husband would be *tall, dark,* and *have good looks.*

Therefore, this sentence is *not* correctly constructed.

Since there are many different grammatical structures in the English language, the possibilities for constructing non-parallel sentences appear to be almost unlimited. Fortunately, you do not have to be able to identify all the grammatical structures in a sentence in order to tell whether or not that sentence has parallel structure. Sentences which lack parallel structure are usually so awkward that they are easy to recognize.

NOT PARALLEL	He worked *quickly, carefully,* and *with steadiness.*
PARALLEL	He worked *quickly, carefully,* and *steadily.*
NOT PARALLEL	He lost weight by *eating* less and *exercised* more.
PARALLEL	He lost weight by *eating* less and *exercising* more.
NOT PARALLEL	The doctor told him *to stop smoking* and *that he should not drink.*
PARALLEL	The doctor told him *to stop smoking* and *drinking.*

Another kind of parallel structure involves the position of correlative conjunctions. **Correlative conjunctions** are conjunctions which occur in pairs, such as:

both . . . and

either . . . or

neither . . . nor

not only . . . but also

Since these conjunctions occur in pairs, they are normally used to compare two ideas. For example:

The refugees had *neither* food *nor* shelter.

The rule for using correlative conjunctions is that the conjunctions *must be placed as closely as possible to the words which are being compared.* For example:

I must *either* cook dinner *or* take my family out to eat.
                              not
I *either* must cook dinner *or* take my family out to eat.

Study the following examples of correctly and incorrectly placed correlative conjunctions.

INCORRECT	During the last three months, my daughter *not only* has had chicken pox *but also* mumps.
CORRECT	During the last three months, my daughter has had *not only* chicken pox *but also* mumps.
INCORRECT	He *both* plays the piano *and* the flute.
CORRECT	He plays *both* the piano *and* the flute.
INCORRECT	She *neither* eats meat *nor* dairy products.
CORRECT	She eats *neither* meat *nor* dairy products.

EXERCISE 22A

Rewrite any sentences which lack parallel structure. If a sentence is already parallel, label it C for *correct*.

1. This school emphasizes the basic skills of reading, how to write, and arithmetic.

   _____

   _____

2. The weather was hot, dry, and with wind blowing.

   _____

   _____

3. Do you know where to meet us and when to be there?

   _____

   _____

4. Fred not only speaks Spanish but also Portuguese.

   _____

   _____

5. He spent his day off playing tennis and went to the beach.

   _____

   _____

6. The policeman asked me to pull over to the curb and that I show him my driver's license.

_____

_____

7. We hope either to go to Italy or to Spain next summer.

_____

_____

8. The household chores which I dislike the most are washing the windows and to mop the floor.

_____

_____

9. He has a tendency to say the wrong thing in the wrong place at a time that is incorrect.

_____

_____

10. Your blind date both is attractive and has intelligence. (There are two errors in this sentence.)

_____

_____

EXERCISE 22B

Rewrite any sentences which lack parallel structure. If a sentence is already parallel, label it *C* for *correct*.

1. Italy has beautiful scenery, delicious food, and the people are friendly.

   _____

   _____

2. The doctor told me that I should stay in bed and to drink a lot of fluids.

   _____

   _____

3. He not only owns a Jaguar but also a Porsche.

   _____

   _____

4. A cantaloupe is ripe when its rind turns yellow, its stem end feels soft, and its seeds rattle.

   _____

   _____

5. The television show was canceled because it had a poor time slot, the acting was bad, and boring stories.

6. I must either get my car lubed today or tomorrow.

7. Tom enjoys playing the guitar and to sing.

8. The steak was tough, overcooked, and had no taste.

9. On the application form, please list your name, where you live, and your phone number.

10. "Neither snow, nor rain, nor heat, nor gloom of night stays these couriers from the swift completion of their appointed rounds." (the inscription on the main branch of the New York City post office)

Capitalization,
Placement of Modifiers,
and Parallel Structure
Unit Review

Part One Add capital letters to the following passage wherever they are needed.

last fall my niece and i spent our thanksgiving vacation in san francisco. we arrived on friday, november 27th, on a united airlines flight from chicago. our aunt gail, who lives north of san francisco in mill valley, met us at the airport.

with the help of a book titled *arthur frommer's guide to san francisco,* we visited many of the city's tourist attractions. on our first day in the city, we rode the powell street cable car to fisherman's wharf, where we had lunch at an italian restaurant called scomas's. then we walked a few blocks west to ghiradelli square. this area used to house a chocolate factory, but the buildings have been converted into shops and restaurants. however, you can still buy a ghiradelli chocolate bar. to end our day, we took a cruise around san francisco bay. the most exciting part of the cruise was passing under the golden gate bridge.

the next day we went to union square, where many of the

city's finest stores are located. we were especially interested in gumps, which sells asian art and artifacts.

from union square it was only a short walk to chinatown, where we had *dim sum* (chinese teacakes) for lunch. we spent the rest of the afternoon buying postcards and souvenirs for our relatives back home in the midwest.

that evening, our aunt and uncle took us to henri's room at the top, a restaurant on the forty-sixth floor of the hilton hotel. as we ate dinner, we had a panoramic view of the city, and we could understand why san francisco is considered to be one of the most beautiful cities in the united states.

Part Two Some of the following sentences contain misplaced or dangling modifiers; others lack parallel structure. Rewrite these incorrect sentences. If a sentence contains no structural errors, label it *C* for *correct*.

1. After an hour of driving around the marina, the restaurant still couldn't be found.

   _____

   _____

2. We made a birthday cake for our daughter's party with chocolate frosting.

   _____

   _____

3. Hoping to make a profit, her money was invested in municipal bonds.

_____

_____

4. The table was set with crystal from Sweden, china from France, and the silverware was made in Italy.

_____

_____

5. Confucianism emphasizes the correct degree of respect between a ruler and his subject, a father and his son, and a husband and his wife.

_____

_____

6. By using a microwave oven, I was able to prepare dinner for six in less than forty-five minutes.

_____

_____

7. A nacho is a fried tortilla chip broiled in an oven covered with cheese and a slice of jalapeño pepper.

_____

_____

8. After the party, he not only had a headache but also indigestion.

_____

_____

9. To run a marathon, a careful training program must be followed.

_____

_____

10. The job requires you to type sixty words a minute and that you take shorthand.

_____

_____

Index

B 0
C 1
D 2
E 3
F 4
G 5
H 6
I 7
J 8